PLANET PERU

PLANET PERU

AN AERIAL JOURNEY THROUGH A TIMELESS LAND

Photographs by
MARILYN BRIDGES

Introduction by
FERNANDO BELAUNDE TERRY

Historical Commentary by
JOHN HYSLOP

Afterword by
MARILYN BRIDGES

THE PROFESSIONAL PHOTOGRAPHY DIVISION OF EASTMAN KODAK COMPANY

APERTURE

To those Peruvians whose ancestors were in touch with the sacred powers of the earth.

ACKNOWLEDGMENTS

With heartfelt gratitude to Ray DeMoulin, general manager-Professional Photography Division and vice president, Eastman Kodak Company, for his unfailing kindness and generous support.

To the Fulbright Commission, for providing the fellowship that allowed this work to begin, and to Marcia Koth de Paredes, director of the Fulbright Commission in Peru, who tried to keep me out of dangerous areas but through no fault of her own did not always succeed.

Without the advice and guidance of certain archaeologists, pilots, guides, and friends, this work would not have been realized: especially, Adriana von Hagen, daughter of the intrepid explorer and writer Victor Wolfgang von Hagen, whose expertise on Peru and enthusiasm for this project proved to be invaluable; Johan Reinhard, author, mountain climber, and anthropologist, who held my ankles as I hung out of a plane's open cargo door over Machu Picchu; and, in alphabetical order, Eduardo Arrarte, the Artadi family, the late Dieter Bauer, David Canal, Fernando Castro, Alfredo Ferreyros, Pascual Garcia, Gaston Garreaud, Carol Mackey, General Jose Nadal, Miguel Pallete, Phyllis Pitluga, Maria Reiche and Renate Reiche, Roberto Rojas, Mauricio de Romaña, Eduardo Ronalds, Olga Samanez, and Helaine Silverman.

To my dear friends and ground support at home: Felicia Murray, Will Peterson, David Blust, Elizabeth Davis; my editors, Thomas Bridges and Andrew Wilkes; and, of course, Michael E. Hoffman, executive director of the Aperture Foundation and publisher of this book.

Library of Congress Catalog Number 91-070511
Hardcover ISBN: 0-89381-469-5

The staff at Aperture for *Planet Peru* is Michael E. Hoffman, Executive Director; Andrew Wilkes, Editor; Jane D. Marsching, Assistant Editor; Susannah Levy, Editorial Work-Scholar; Stevan Baron, Production Director; Linda Tarack, Production Associate.

Project Editor: Thomas Bridges

Translator: Maria Lamadrid

Captions by Adriana von Hagen

Book design by Paul Hardy

Aperture Foundation, Inc., publishes a periodical, books, and portfolios of fine photography to communicate with serious photographers and creative people everywhere. A complete catalog is available upon request. Address: 20 East 23rd Street, New York, New York 10010.

Photographs: p. 2, Eroded Adobe, Túcume, 1988; pp. 4-5, Porters, Inka Trail, 1988; pp. 6-7, Desert Military Installation, Pisco Valley, 1989.

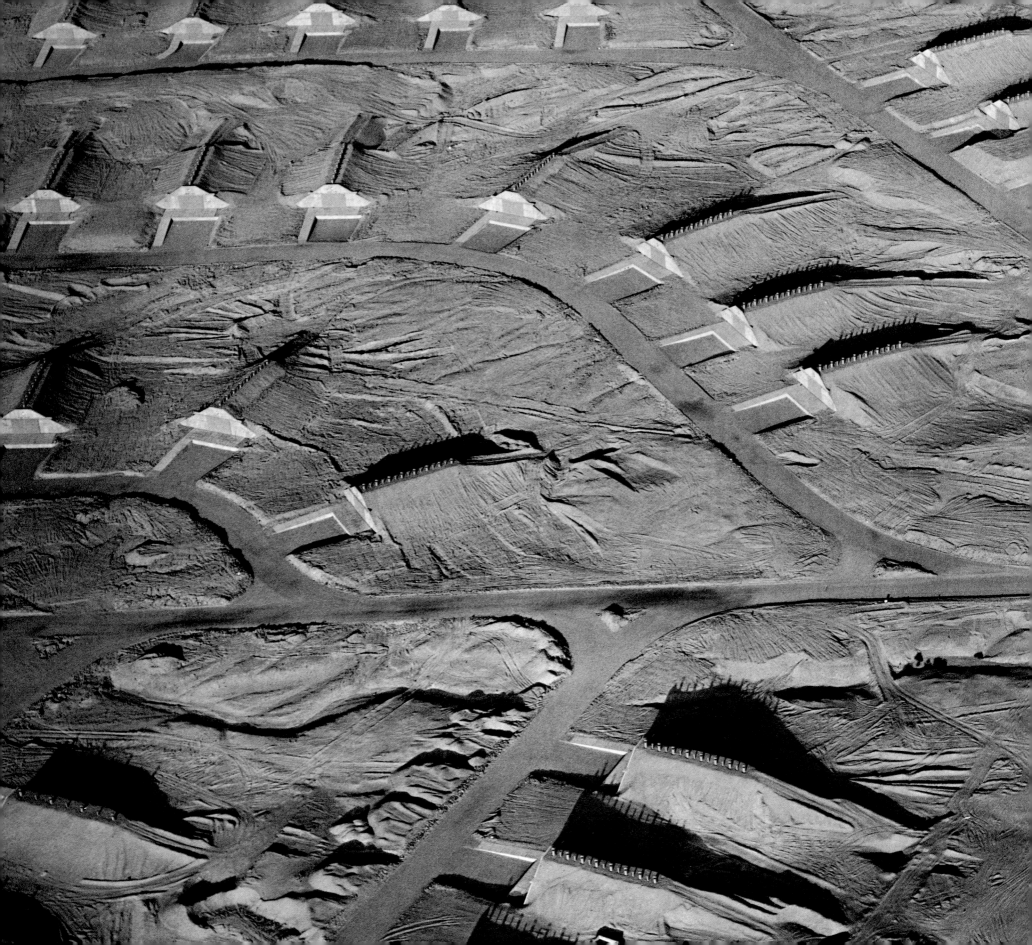

CONTENTS

INTRODUCTION

By Fernando Belaúnde Terry

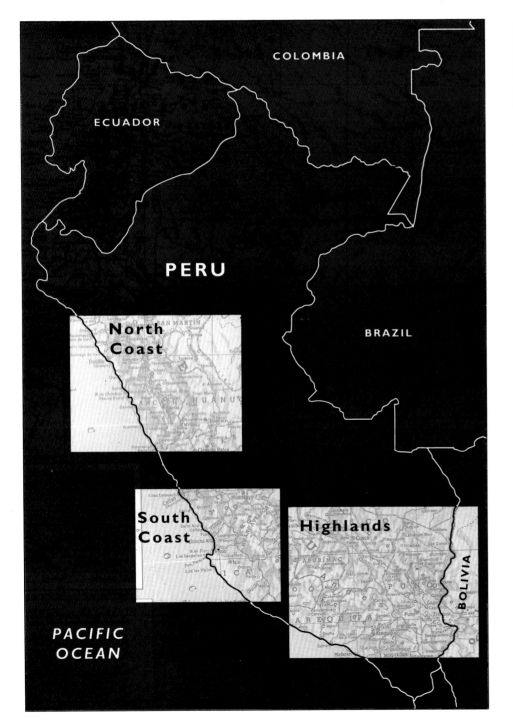

L ike the Andean condor, Marilyn Bridges has agile wings and penetrating eyes. Her book *Planet Peru* would have been impossible without her extraordinary ability to hover above her objectives and capture them with a lens of exceptional fidelity.

Combining a unique sensitivity to both geography and archaeology, this artist performs "vertical exploration" rather than a much less expansive "horizontal exploration," which would limit her interpretation of such important legacies as the monumental lines and designs on the pampas of Nazca.

Before the advent of hot-air balloons, used during wartime to detect troop movement, all topographical observations were made from the ground, or from the horizontal vantage point of the sea, or, in some cases, from mountain lookouts. The development of aeronautics broadened the scope of vertical exploration. With the great advance in aerial photographic technology, a veritable revolution in cartography occurred, speeding the development of topographical surveys, including relief maps. The Peruvian government established such a mapping service in 1929.

The historic Shippee-Johnson exploration of the 1930s, an incipient event in Peruvian aerial photography, left a documentation of various archaeological sites that facilitated the study of our past, but this survey lacked the artistic sensibility and dedication to form found in *Planet Peru*.

Eventually, the conquest of space would come to perfect most precisely the mastery of universal geography. Through the use of remote sensors, by way of satellites stationed hundreds of miles in the sky, scientists achieved a miraculous view of our entire planet, detecting natural resources on both land and sea. What a remarkable evolution has ensued from the imperfect horizontal exploration glimpsed from the vantage point of galleons at sea to the flawless vertical observation now possible from satellites!

The work of Marilyn Bridges, with her dual mastery of camera

(Right) Moray, 1989. Limestone sinkholes terraced by the Inkas above the Urubamba Valley, northwest of Cuzco.

8

and airplane, holds a privileged position between those two extremes. It confirms Oscar Wilde's assertion that *"the artist always has been and always will be a marvelous exception."* From high above we see legendary Peru, this immense cemetery of dead cities, this land of sparks of genius and of unfinished works.

Geology, painting, and sculpture merge in Bridges' view of the volcanoes in the region of the Colca Valley, an antediluvian river valley surrounded by canyons whose monumental proportions surpass those of the Colorado River to such a degree that they might be imagined as fantastic fiction. As far as I know, no one but Bridges has viewed these volcanoes at a moment of greater radiance, capturing with such intensity the reflective surfaces as

Pouring pisco, above Ollantaytambo, 1988. A *puna* (highland) tradition calls for an offering to Pachamama (earth mother) before consuming pisco, a fiery liquor made from grapes.

they seem to shimmer at will. Picturesque fragments of agriculture and extraordinary ancient terracing are also imprinted by her camera. Not a single straight line is found in the terracing; instead, everything follows natural topographical contours, a faithful reflection of the landscape.

Machu Picchu—"the Lost City of the Inkas"—has been photographed from every angle thousands of times. But Bridges' artistic sensibility brings it into focus from above in order to achieve a play of light and shadow *"in the Cyclopean fury of the Andes,"* as Pablo Neruda would say. She exposes a miraculous reflection that presents a city created without profaning or damaging the topography, instead caressing it and leaving proof of love and respect for nature. Why was such a site chosen? Because, it was decided, one philosopher has said, that *"the soul needs more space than the body."*

As Neruda said of artists, *"I come to speak for your mute mouths,"* so Bridges could say of these miraculous images, *"I come to see for your closed eyes. . . ."*

Bridges' eclectic eye is never diminished, and she never fails to stimulate our imagination. We view the curvilinear terracing of Moray—that remote experimental agricultural station of pre-Columbian America—which shows an ancient inclination toward organic planning in the methodology of its land use. And at Chinchero, where agricultural planning is barely interrupted by impassable geographic obstacles, we see the rationalistic approach to ordering that man inevitably imposes on the terrain. What a fascinating invitation to philosophic discussion these captured vistas contain!

Through her imagery, one must feel the rapture in Bridges' heart as she observes from the altitude of the condor these wonderful displays of landscape as they become prey for her camera. Among her photographs there is a panoramic vision of dunes that invade everything in the coastal desert. It is like a picture of the wind. This Aeolian force, disregarding the work of man, obstructs even the Pan American Highway. The desert imposes itself according to the will of nature. In still another photograph, we see a beautiful version of an oasis, not far from the necropolis of Paracas, in the extraordinary image of the Huacachina resort, surrounding a small lake, much like an emerald in sand.

A mere glance at the ancient fields of Atiquipa is enough to confirm Hyams' definition of the ancient Peruvians: *a people who were a builder of lands.* And how can one but marvel at the mystery contained in a view of the slopes of the Pisco Valley, which shows along the edge of a buttress a monumental line made up of an infinity of wells lined with stone that forms an immense network of human constructions whose function is yet to be de-

Wiñay Wayna, 1988. Wiñay Wayna's estimated eighty terraces, flight of fountains, and finely built granite walls suggest that it was an important ritual stopping point, the last of several such sites on the Inka Trail before reaching Machu Picchu.

termined. Were they perhaps warehouses to preserve the harvest in more suitable climate at a higher altitude?

The monumental planned city of Chan Chan is well known because of its proximity to the Trujillo airport. But it is not for this accident of modern planning that it attracts the attention of Bridges. Here, Bridges postulates on urban planning of the past. Her view demonstrates a conception of visionary planning that predates what centuries later would come to be called the "super city block"; that is to say, a self-sufficient rectangular unity that surpasses in extension, population, and facilities what a simple 100-meter-by-100-meter city block can offer as a basic modular unit for a city. It may be because adobe seems less stringent and more humanistic than steel, brick, and glass, but there appears to be a sense of symmetry and linear balance at Chan Chan that is not found in most modern construction.

Although less explored, the dead city of Pacatnamú at the sea's edge in the valley of Jequetepaque demonstrates the grandiose nature of its urban grouping and continues to invite exploratory research. Even enveloped as it is in the debris of landslides, its original urban conception is not obscured. And further, at Túcume, to the far north, the clarity of Bridges' photographic lens yields a dramatic expression of ancient urban construction, the expanse of which was unmatched in the hemisphere.

Finally, in contrast with the Great Wall of China, which follows topographical contours, the Great Wall of Peru, in the valley of the Santa River, shows its clear rectangular lines in the middle of the most haphazard topography. Here humanity imposed conditions on nature. Modern instruments could not improve on the delineation.

In *Planet Peru,* Marilyn Bridges observes the epidermis of Peru, replete with scars, some long set and almost invisible to less acute vision. Peru remains a mysterious country. Bridges' important and sensitive photographs will, it is to be hoped, act as a catalyst to tempt investigators to search for other unexposed treasures from Peru's past.

HIGHLANDS

By John Hyslop

When time still lingered in a void and was yet to relate to man, the Creator, who the Inkas called Wirakocha, resided and created all things at a place called Tiwanaku.[1] From there, he ordered the sun, moon, and stars to an island in Lake Titicaca and deemed that it was from here that they would rise daily into the heavens. At a great rock on the island, the sun appeared in the form of a light-enveloped man and spoke to the astonished Inkas, who were then a fledgling people as yet without destiny. To one of their number, Manco Qhapaq, the sun addressed the following prophecy before ascending into the heavens with the moon and stars: *"You and your descendants are destined to conquer many lands and people, and be great lords. Always hold me as your father, taking pride in being my children, without ever forgetting me."*

During the fifteenth century, when the Inkas, who still comprised a small kingdom in the southern highlands of Peru, had begun building an empire, this myth and a host of others would be used to further their claim that Inka authority to rule over mankind came from the most sanctified of entities, the Sun itself. Tribute to their fundamental benefactor was the basis of the Inka state religion, a solar cult, and the Inka sanctuary at Lake Titicaca was one of the most hallowed places in the Andes. Manco Qhapaq stepped from the shadows of myth and was regarded as the first Inka.

During the century that preceded the Spanish Conquest, the Inkas did indeed seem favored by the gods. Beginning about 1450, Inka armies swept over the highlands and deserts of the Andes and rapidly assembled an empire that encompassed numerous kingdoms and small ethnic groups. A diverse population of perhaps fourteen million people was being forged into a unified state.

When the Spanish conquistador Francisco Pizarro and his band of 168 *tercios* entered the domain of the Inkas in 1532 in zealous pursuit of legendary riches, they could hardly have imagined the extent and sophistication of the empire they had begun to penetrate.

TAWANTINSUYU

The Empire was called Tawantinsuyu, or the "Land of the Four Parts." It stretched nearly 2,600 miles, the distance across the continental United States, extending along the mountains from the present Colombian-Ecuadoran border to a point just south of Santiago, Chile.

Bounded by the Pacific Ocean on the west and tropical forests on the east, few preindustrial states have encompassed such a wide

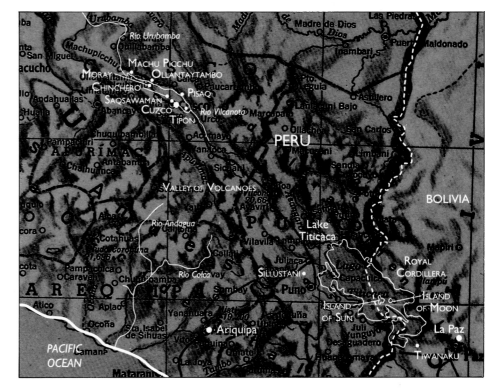

---

[1] A number of words in this text are in the Inka language, often referred to as *Quechua*. Several such words here are spelled differently than in the past, including the word Inka (Inca). They utilize a new orthography that more accurately represents sounds in Quechua. These modern spellings permit the Inka tongue to become a more exact instrument of written communication.

(Left) Twin cinder cones, Andagua Valley, 1989.

(Left) Alpacas, 1988. Alpacas, llamas, and European sheep graze together on high Andean plateaus. (Far left) Statuary, Tiwanaku, 1989.

range of environments. The Andean slopes included verdant valleys and lush, humid jungles. Volcanoes and massive mountain ranges crowned the Inka state from north to south. The highlands ranged from rainy grasslands in the north to arid plateaus in the south and sheltered agricultural valleys of rich cultivated fields and high plains where llamas and alpacas were herded, providing sustenance for millions of people. The Pacific coast of the Empire from Ecuador to Chile was a desert, crosscut by dozens of rivers descending from the Andes. On these broad irrigated deserts, civilized people had thrived for millenia.

Much Inka technology was heavily influenced by the ecology of the Andes. Terracing of the Andean slopes, although pre-Inka in origin, was continued by the Inkas, greatly increasing the agricultural yield. In the region of Lake Titicaca, raised fields surrounded by water, *camellones,* converted parts of the high plateau into rich agricultural zones. Vast irrigation projects also ensured the fertility of both highland and desert terrains.

The Inka Empire had been assembled by skillful warfare and brilliant diplomacy, and it was held together by political savvy using a diversity of governing tactics.

The Inka language, *Quechua,* was fostered as a unifying lingua franca. State colonists from Cuzco and elsewhere were moved throughout the Empire for economic development and political control. The Cult of the Sun was propagated in all assimilated territories, although non-Inka deities were often tolerantly incorporated in the Inka pantheon.

A road system of more than fourteen thousand miles bound the disparate parts of the state together. These roadways facilitated the distribution of products and the movement of state officials. Ingenious devices, such as great staircases of thousands of steps, were used to ascend mountains.

Much governance of the Empire was left to the local non-Inka lords. The regional rulers and their families were enculturated into Inka ways by frequent required visits to Cuzco, where their children were educated. Local lords throughout the Andes accepted imperial gifts of Inka women as wives, with the result that their children, future lords of the Empire, were part Inka. Some of these lords became very loyal subjects and willingly adopted many aspects of Inka culture. On the high plateau around Lake Titicaca, the imposing towers of their burial buildings, *chulpas,* constructed with fine Inka masonry, still punctuate the horizons on the grasslands where herds of llamas and alpacas leisurely graze.

Thus far, the portrait of the Inka Empire would seem to reach utopian dimensions, but, as history shows us, the résumé of any successful state is punctuated by divisive elements as well as cohesive bonds. These weaknesses, and fate, would prove tragic for the young Inka Empire.

By November 1532, Pizarro and his small force had ascended the Andes to the Inka city of Cajamarca in the northern highlands. Just outside the city, the Inka Emperor, Atawalpa, and his accompanying court of thousands was camped, along with an army of some twenty to thirty thousand battle-savvy warriors. In a lightning move of entrapment, Pizarro and his men bodily seized the Emperor and massacred a substantial portion of his thunderstruck court. The demoralized army fled the iconoclastic foreigners.

Yet, in spite of traditional misconceptions, Francisco Pizarro's successful campaign was not alone the result of superior military strategy or prowess. It was the conquistador's overwhelming good fortune to find the Empire in the final throes of a civil war of succession.

The Empire suffered from debilitating factors that have plagued other large states. Internecine warfare wracked the Empire in times of imperial succession as royal lineages fought for power. At the same time, many of the incorporated ethnic groups recalled a past when they were independent and thus were loyal Inka subjects only superficially. Indeed, the Spanish conquerors were aided by several of these disgruntled Andean groups.

The rapid Inka expansion had created such a geographically

extensive polity that its administration was increasingly cumbersome. A system of imperial messengers, *chaski,* could shuffle messages throughout the state in days or weeks on its road system, but rebellions or incursions by uncivilized tribes took years to deal with, since armies were marshaled and moved slowly.

Finally, the Inka concern with expansion had led to chronic warfare on several of its borders with little result. In its last decades, the treasury of the great state—its manpower and resources—were expended in years of fruitless militarism.

Given more time, the Inka unifying strategies should have overcome many of the weaknesses and made the nascent Empire less precarious. And one must wonder whether the Inkas might not have achieved a long-lived state if the European invasion had not forever altered Andean destiny.

Men knitting in small village plaza, Taquile Island, Lake Titicaca, 1988.

LAKE TITICACA AND CUZCO

Lake Titicaca and the region around it had profound significance in Inka religious tradition because of associations with primal origins and the principal deity in Inka worship, the Sun. At some 13,000 feet in altitude and 3,500 square miles in area, it is the highest lake of its size in the world. It is also astonishingly beautiful. Its waters shimmer with light, mirroring the sweep of the sky with such breadth that it seems to turn the world upside down. Here, the Island of the Sun, with its venerated sanctuary, rests in an environment of overwhelming power. Even the modern visitor would be indeed insensitive not to grasp intuitively the integration of Inka religious concepts with the natural environment.

South of Lake Titicaca lies the site of the great city of Tiwanaku, once seat of an empire that flourished between A.D. 200 and 1100 and spread its domain over much of Bolivia and parts of Chile. Already abandoned at the time the Inkas rose to power, it became associated in Inka myth as the home of Wirakocha and the point of creation. Tiwanaku's colossal stonework is rivaled only by later Inka creations.

Although in ruins, the Inka sanctuary at Lake Titicaca is still considered sacred (in part because it has been transformed into a Christian shrine). It was once one of the most revered spots in the Empire. Early historical sources claim it was rivaled only by Cuzco and by Pachacamac, the great pilgrimage and oracle center on the Pacific coast. Early European visitors reported more than six hundred attendants at the shrine, and allegedly a thousand women brewed corn beer as a libation that was poured over the Sacred Rock. That outcrop, from which the sun was said to have appeared to the original Inkas, is still a prominent feature, although now bereft of the silver and metal plates that, tradition records, once adorned it. From here, the sun's rays were said to have been reflected in a blaze of light that could be seen from the lake's distant shores.

The sacred inferences attached to Lake Titicaca were matched by the significance of the Inka capital, Cuzco. In Cuzco, the In-

(Left) Chulpa, Sillustani, 1989. The Qolla elite near Lake Titicaca built these stone burial towers, 9 to 40 feet in height, between the 12th and 14th centuries A.D. (Far left) Camellones, Lake Titicaca, 1988. These raised fields date back to approximately 1000 B.C.

kas created a city that symbolized and reflected the world as they conceived it. Foremost, its center was reserved for the Inkas. Immense rectangular buildings surrounded three sides of a large plaza, and surrounding this core were fine masonry enclosures called *kancha,* which provided space for Inka royal lineages and their retainers. Some enclosures housed temples to various deities, while others were the residence and work space of specially chosen women, *aqlla,* who performed particular tasks for the state such as spinning, weaving, and preparing the cherished corn beer, *chicha,* used in large quantities for both feasts and libations. Many roads connected Cuzco to its hinterland, but four main ones extended out from the city's center to the four quarters of the Empire.

Surrounding the center zone, there were approximately a dozen districts where lords and others from all parts of the Empire were in residence. Thus the city became a microcosm of the Empire, with Inkas and non-Inkas alike residing together according to a symbolic urban design. It is uncertain how many people lived in Cuzco, but estimates indicate that it was in excess of one hundred thousand, a city as large as any in Europe at the time.

One can still admire the remains of many Inka walls and edifices in central Cuzco, but one building complex, Saqsawaman, in the north of the city, stands out as a unique architectural achievement, above comparison to anything else in South America.

The immense religious-military complex of Saqsawaman, designed and constructed by the Inkas across many acres on a hill overlooking the city, astounded the first Europeans to view it in the sixteenth century. Three immense zigzag terrace walls were its most striking feature. These formidable structures were made with massive stones, some weighing upward of one hundred tons, and precisely fitted together with no mortar bond. The high walls reminded the early Spanish of a fortress, but later, more accurate informants noted that both the walls and its central building were used for solar worship, important festivals, and the storage of great quantities of luxury commodities and military supplies. Two high towers, now demolished, one round and one rectangular, crowned the top of the majestic complex.

One particularly astute Spaniard, the chronicler Cieza de León, was in Cuzco in the 1540s and recorded information about the building of Saqsawaman. Cieza wrote that an Inka Emperor "ordered twenty thousand men sent in from the provinces, and that the villages supply men with the necessary food. . . . These Indians were not permanently engaged in this work, but only for a limited time, and then others came and they left, so the work did not become onerous. Four thousand of them quarried and cut the stones; six thousand hauled them with great cables of leather and hemp; the others dug the ditch and laid the foundation, while still others cut poles and beams for the timbers."

Unfortunately, the Spanish occupation of Cuzco in the sixteenth century resulted in the removal of many of Saqsawaman's smaller stones for construction of Spanish buildings and churches in Cuzco. But the great terrace walls were so monumental that they remained to some degree impervious. Like the pyramids of Egypt or the Great Wall of China, Saqsawaman was simply too immense for destructive, unappreciative later generations to desecrate.

THE EMPIRE AND ITS ANTECEDENTS

The Inka Empire could not have been assembled without more than two millennia of advanced Andean cultural development. The Andes are one of the few areas of the world, together with China, the Near East, and Mexico, where civilization emerged independently from simpler, less complex societies.

Although debate continues as to just when and how civilized life was first achieved in the Andes, it is generally acknowledged that it occurred in the first or second millennium before Christ. Therefore, the Inkas must be observed as the culmination, not the origin, of a long tradition of Andean civilized life. This point

is fundamental to understanding the Inka achievement, which was not to "civilize" the Andes but to mold its peoples into a single state.

The Inkas saw it differently. They believed their state was a civilizing force that brought order and peace to a chaotic region. They did not know that numerous states had risen and fallen, and empires had extended their sway, many times before in the Andes. Had they known, the Inkas might have incorporated more of these ancient peoples into a vision of the past world that justified both their existence and their sovereignty. The Inkas, as we understand them, were quite capable of manipulating history.

In fact, many of the great cultural achievements once attributed solely to the Inkas (by the Inkas as well as by those who first studied them) are now known to have been well under way long before their rise to power. Notable examples are the outstanding

Monoliths, Ollantaytambo, 1988. Six huge monoliths formed part of the Inka sun temple at Ollantaytambo, one of Emperor Pachakuti's royal estates in the Urubamba Valley.

irrigation projects in the Pacific coastal deserts and the development of complex road networks. Imposing ceremonial centers and secular strongholds also had been constructed for at least two thousand years before the Inkas.

Perhaps the most visually striking and labor-intensive feat of pre-Inka peoples was the terracing of the Andes. In their quest to create more arable land, earlier civilizations had transformed the Andean slopes into tremendous stepped surfaces supported by infinite numbers of stone retention walls. Throughout the sierra of Peru, the most bewildering displays of terracing, often on the most precipitous mountains, are observed. Some of the best examples are in the remote Colca Valley in southern Peru, where the efforts of countless individuals over centuries converted a rugged natural topography into a totally humanized environment. For miles and miles, mountain slopes of the most formidable inclines have been transformed into tiered webs of functional and exquisitely beautiful terracing.

INKA RELIGION AND THE SACRED LANDSCAPE

The religion of the Inkas was so complex that no scholar as yet has been able to put together confidently a comprehensive description of it. Sacred activities permeated many areas of human endeavor that we consider primarily secular, such as agriculture, architecture, and even warfare. The Inka Sun cult was predominant throughout Tawantinsuyu, and the Inka king was considered a descendent or son of the Sun. Various celestial phenomena were considered sacred; among them the moon was of primary importance. Meteorological entities such as thunder, rain, and lightning also were worshiped. Wirakocha, the creator deity, was associated with primal waters, especially the sea and lakes, and its many aspects made for a most ambiguous god. Many traditional facets of Andean religions, common to many peoples other than the Inkas, were continued and even propagated by the Inkas. A prime example of such a pan-Andean religious tradition is the sanctification of natural objects and landscape.

Andean and Inka religion was highly animistic and considered many natural phenomena sacred. Mountains were worshiped for their relationship to fertility and rainfall. Sanctuaries were built on dozens of volcanoes and mountains and furnished with offerings of the finest textiles, elegant metal and shell figurines, and even sacrificed children. Still today, after 450 years of Christian domination, many Andean peoples continue to hold their mountains sacred.

Many Andean groups believed their primal origin was linked to natural phenomena. Boulders and outcrops, and springs and rivers, became hallowed places where offerings and sacrifices took place and where rituals were regularly performed. Boulders were often carved with shelves for offerings and with channels for libations. Water sources were adorned with basins and channels of the finest masonry. In Inka settlements, elegant waterworks were built primarily for ritual purposes.

The sanctification of the environment by Andean peoples may be difficult for many modern observers to conceive. The Inkas believed that earthly objects and landforms related spiritually to the prosperity of their herds, the success of their agriculture, the welfare of their families and leaders, and success in war. The sacred landscape also was a means of recalling a mythical and historical past. Boulders represented mythical heroes, and specific terrains brought to memory ancient battles and valorous events. Springs, canals, and rivers related to the fundamental Creator's association with the sea and lakes. Other aspects of nature symbolized important mythical animals in the form of felines and snakes.

Thus Andean and Inka peoples saw much of the natural world as both animated and sacred. A seventeenth-century Spanish observer in Cuzco spoke of the mysteries present in and the veneration of "every hill, spring, road, and canyon." One cannot begin to comprehend the nature of Inka architecture and settlement planning without seriously taking into account the role of the sacred landscape.

INKA ARCHITECTURE AND LANDSCAPE ENGINEERING

The Spaniards were able to loot only the Inkas' portable wealth. But in an ironic twist, much of the Inkas' most complex and spectacular material legacy—their architectural planning—has survived.

The Inkas created thousands of settlements throughout their Empire, but some of the most extraordinary are concentrated in the Cuzco region, the Inka heartland. Several of these, such as Pisaq, Ollantaytambo, and Machu Picchu, are located along the Vilcanota-Urubamba river valley north of Cuzco. One part of this valley system, a section near Cuzco, was known as the Sacred

Intiwatana, Pisaq, 1988. The religious sector at Pisaq, a former Inka royal estate in the Vilcanota Valley, offers some of the finest examples of Inka masonry in the Cuzco area. The curved wall structure (center) surrounds an elaborately carved rock.

(Right) Ollantaytambo, 1989. This is the oldest continuously occupied settlement in the Andes and the site of a bloody battle in 1536 between Spanish forces and rebel Inkas. (Far right) Inka wall and colonial church tower, Chinchero, 1988.

Valley and has an especially noteworthy concentration of stonework and terraces. In higher regions around Cuzco are other important settlements, such as Tipón and Chinchero. These, and the aforementioned Sacred Valley sites, were royal estates and symbols of the state. There, Inka kings, their descendants and their lieges, lived in splendor, pursued a ritualized life, and engaged in leisurely activities such as the hunt.

These noble retreats are for several reasons illustrative of many aspects of Inka religious and symbolic thought. The Inka elite in the Cuzco area controlled the wealth of the Empire—the manpower—that was necessary for the time-consuming landscape engineering and stone masonry typical of many settlements. Workers from throughout the state were imported to man the quarries and laboriously move, shape, and fit the massive stones that were the building blocks of Inka architecture. Armies of laborers shifted tons of earth to form terraces for architectural complexes and ritual crops. Rivers were straightened and canalized, a truly monumental task. Nature in its pristine form was transformed into a new reality that, in Inka eyes, ennobled the landscape. No New World civilization manipulated and transformed the landscape to the degree carried out by the Inkas.

It would be a grave error to consider Inka landscape engineering similar to that of the modern world. Whereas aesthetic considerations may have been important, the motivations of Inka engineers and architects were embedded in highly developed concepts about the sacred natural world. Important outcrops and boulders, each with specific meaning, were integrated into buildings and terrace walls.

Ritually important agricultural terraces transformed the landscape from irregular curves and slopes into a fine geometry of steps, regular curves, and horizontal and vertical planes. The magnificent terraces at Machu Picchu, Chinchero, Tipón, Moray, Ollantaytambo, and Pisaq attest to the scope of Inka landscape design. All could have been equally productive with far less landscape engineering and simpler masonry, but they were en-grandized because it was at these sites that Inka royalty performed agricultural rituals that benefited the entire state. Crops of ritual importance, primarily corn and coca, were carefully tended for religious reasons far beyond their harvest's nutritional value. It is notable how the elegant terraces are an integral part of the human settlements and are as much a part of Inka architecture as the buildings themselves.

No Inka settlement so well illustrates these concepts as the enigmatic Machu Picchu. This superbly preserved settlement justifiably has become an icon of the most highly developed Inka beliefs relating to architecture, natural objects, and sacred landscape. At least two dozen important boulders are integrated into its design, along with a complex ritual water system of interconnected baths and fountains. The irregular topography has been terraced for buildings and agriculture. The site is intimate with its natural surroundings, resting within a panorama of rugged peaks and nearly surrounded by a verdant gorge. The sacred role of the mountains surrounding the remains of Machu Picchu is still recalled by the area's native residents.

Much of Inka landscape engineering invites speculation that its builders were guided by or were aware of an aerial perspective. Nearby or even distant mountains easily could have been observation points before, during, and after construction. Thus the aerial perspectives presented in the photographs here may truly enhance a visual conception the Inkas wished to convey.

Agurto Calvo, Santiago. *Estudios acerca de la construcción, arquitectura, y planeamiento incas*, Instituto Nacional de Cultura del Perú, Cuzco, 1987.

Cobo, Bernabé. *Historia del Nuevo Mundo*, (1653), Biblioteca de Autores Españoles, vols. 91–92, Atlas, Madrid, 1964.

Cieza de León, Pedro de. *The Incas*, (1553), ed. Victor W. von Hagen, trans. Harriet de Onis, University of Oklahoma Press, Norman, 1959.

Hemming, John. *The Conquest of the Incas*, Harcourt Brace Jovanovich, Inc., New York, 1970.

Hyslop, John. *The Inka Road System*, Academic Press, New York and San Francisco, 1984.

———. *Inka Settlement Planning*, University of Texas Press, Austin, 1990.

ISLAND OF THE SUN FROM THE WEST, Lake
Titicaca, 1989. The Inka sanctuary on the Island of the
Sun, one of the holiest in the Empire, was an important
pilgrimage center. Origin myths link the legendary
founders of the Inka Empire, Manco Qhapaq and his
sister consort, Mama Ocllo, and the Sun God, Inti, the
supreme Inka deity, to a sacred rock outcrop on the
six-mile-long island.

ISLAND OF THE SUN FROM NORTHEAST, Lake Titicaca, 1989. After the Inkas conquered the Lake Titicaca region in the mid-15th century A.D., they built temples dedicated to Inti and lesser deities—the moon, stars, thunder, and rainbow—on the island. The sacred rock (center) was covered with finely woven cloth and sheets of gold that reflected the rays of the sun.

TIWANAKU, 1989. The world's highest ancient urban center (some 12,690 feet above sea level) and the center of a long-lived empire in the Andes, Tiwanaku lies southeast of Lake Titicaca in what is now Bolivia. Flourishing between A.D. 200 and 1100, Tiwanaku once controlled areas of southern Peru, northern Chile, and Bolivia. At its height, around A.D. 500, Tiwanaku's architects built the massive Akapana mound (top, right), the Kalasasaya temple (center), and a semisubterranean temple (above Kalasasaya). Already in ruins at the time of the Inkas' rise to power, Tiwanaku was deemed the residence of the creator-god Wirakocha in Inka myths.

SAQSAWAMAN, OVERLOOKING CUZCO,
1989. The religious-military complex of Saqsawaman
has overlooked the former Inka capital of Cuzco for
nearly five centuries. When first seen by the Spaniards
in 1533, Cuzco housed a population of some 100,000,
and was the largest city in South America. Although
Inka mythology attributes Cuzco's founding to Manco
Qhapaq in time immemorial, it was remodeled into an
imperial city by the Inka Pachakuti in the early 15th
century. Modern Cuzco remains a partially Indian city,
retaining aspects of its original settlement pattern and
many Inka walls.

VALLEY OF THE VOLCANOES #1, Andagua, 1989. The Andagua Valley is known as the Valley of the Volcanoes because of a series of more than eighty cinder cones, ranging from 50 to 250 feet in height, that pockmark the basaltic covering of the river valley. The ancient inhabitants of the nearby valleys attributed their own origins to volcanoes.

VALLEY OF THE VOLCANOES #2, Andagua,
1989. The cinder cones were formed when gas and air
trapped in lava flows from eruptions of volcanoes in
prehistoric times exploded upon their release, creating a
progeny of miniature volcanoes.

CABANACONDE, Colca Valley, 1989. According
to legend, the Colca Valley was first inhabited by
Cabana (Quechua-speaking) and Collagua (Aymara-
speaking) peoples, each settling in respective sections of
the river valley. In the middle of the 15th century
A.D., the Inkas conquered the area.

VILLAGE OF MADRIGAL, Colca Valley, 1989.
Located on the right bank of the Colca River and
flanked by terracing, Madrigal dates to the late 16th
century A.D., when the Spanish conquistador
Francisco Pizarro granted land to his loyal followers
and more than a dozen Spanish-style villages grew up
along the valley.

29

VILLAGE OF LARI, Colca Valley, 1989. The villages of the remote Colca Valley remained largely forgotten until aerial reconnaissance rediscovered them in the 1930s. Lari's 18th-century church and central plaza form the centerpiece for a grid plan of streets and building lots of Spanish origin. In recent times, unscrupulous collectors of religious icons have stripped the churches of their lavish ornaments.

TERRACING, Madrigal, Colca Valley, 1989. An elaborate web of stone agricultural terracing watered by irrigation-canal networks frames the Colca Valley. The ancient agricultural system remains an effective means for the Collaguas to grow their crops of wheat, barley, and especially native maize, for which the valley is famed.

SACRED LAKE, near Chinchero, 1989. The Inkas
viewed lakes as sacred and often made offerings to
water sources believed to be connected with rainfall.
Water was a primary symbol of fertility and origin to
the Inkas. Fundamental to their beliefs, and to some
extent those of the Andean peoples as a whole, was the
concept that water surrounded the world and lay
beneath it.

JAGGED WALLS, Saqsawaman, 1989. The huge, 1,000-foot-long zigzag walls of Saqsawaman present a defensive posture, but they probably relate to religious symbolism rather than military prowess. In the 15th century A.D., an Inka emperor ordered his architects to build the complex, and more than 20,000 men labored for decades, often hauling massive stones weighing up to 100 tons from quarries miles away. Two towers, one round and one rectangular (all destroyed), overlooked the wide esplanade of the complex, which may have served as a "House of the Sun" as well as an armory.

KENQO, 1989. This carved limestone outcrop near Saqsawaman is riddled with caves and carvings and was once a shrine sited on a *zeque* line, the conceptual set of lines radiating from the Korikancha, Inka Cuzco's most sacred building. A small semicircular plaza with the remains of nineteen niches lies on one side of the outcrop and faces a sacred, upright stone surrounded by a platform wall. A cave inside the outcrop has an altarlike carving.

SUCHUNA, Saqsawaman, 1989. Saqsawaman's Suchuna sector, which lies just to the north of the complex's main plaza, was partially uncovered by archaeologists in 1985. It was found to be replete with aqueducts, cisterns, terraces, patios, stairs, buildings, and a so-called Throne of the Inka that consists of a set of sculpted shelves in bedrock. The site also includes a large reservoir that once supplied water to Cuzco and had ritual functions as well. The Spanish, eager to obliterate all traces of Inka religion, ordered that more than 2,000 llama-loads of dirt be hauled in to cover up the reservoir and its related cisterns and canals.

PISAQ, 1989. Located in the temperate Vilcanota Valley northeast of Cuzco, Pisaq was one of the royal estates of the Emperor Pachakuti. Agricultural terraces sweep down the hillside to the valley floor. Fine masonry rooms characterize the *Intiwatana* religious sector, which includes a curved building surrounding a rock outcrop and a ritual water system.

MACHU PICCHU AND URUBAMBA RIVER, 1989. Perched almost a mile above the gorge of the Urubamba River, Machu Picchu's remote setting led American explorer Hiram Bingham to believe he had stumbled upon the lost capital of the Inkas when he discovered the ruins in 1911. Although the Spanish conquistadors never reached Machu Picchu, 16th-century land-tenure documents reveal that it may have been a royal estate of the Emperor Pachakuti, who reigned in the mid-15th century, and not the fabled hidden capital.

MACHU PICCHU, 1989. A series of plazas divides the religious precinct, including a circular building of fine masonry, from the residential sector to the east (right). The citadel probably never housed more than 1,000 people, judging from its 200 dwellings. Its population included priests, administrators, and agricultural laborers who cultivated maize and other crops on the agricultural terraces surrounding the site. A chain of sixteen spring-fed water catchments supplied water for ritual purposes. An on-site quarry provided the Inka stonemasons with granite blocks to build Machu Picchu's finely wrought walls.

MACHU PICCHU AMONG THE PEAKS OF
THE ANDES, 1989. Machu Picchu's spectacular
cloud-forest setting surrounded by sacred peaks added
to its importance as a religious center. Its inaccessible
location, defensive walls, and dry moat probably
served to limit access to the religious precinct rather
than deter would-be invaders.

MORAY AND PLAIN, 1989. These circular
agricultural terraces, built by the Inkas in natural
sinkholes on a limestone plateau, overlook the
Urubamba Valley some fifteen miles northwest of
Cuzco. Unique in the Andes, it has been suggested that
they have cosmological meaning and even that they
served as amphitheaters. Their function, if other than
agricultural, however, remains a mystery.

MORAY FROM THE PERPENDICULAR, 1989. A
research team in the early 1980s found that temperature
fluctuations among the terrace levels in the sinkholes
created up to twenty distinct ecosystems and speculated
that the Inkas may have used the site for agricultural
experiments. Research may further explore this
proposition.

CHINCHERO, 1989. Built as a royal estate by Thupa
Inka (ca. 1471–1493), Chinchero lies on the fertile
potato-growing high plain between Cuzco and the
Urubamba Valley. A large plaza ends in finely built
terraces that once sustained crops watered by a
complex canal system. Elaborately carved stone
outcrops are situated throughout the area. The Spanish
built their town over the Inka settlement.

TIPON, 1989. Tipón lies some ten miles southeast of Cuzco and contains some of the finest agricultural terracing ever built in the Cuzco area. The elaborate terracing network, lined with stone walls, gives prominence to the site and suggests that it might have been a royal estate. Crops were watered by a cistern connected by a stone-lined aqueduct to terraces complete with elaborate channels and fountains.

MOUTH OF THE VOLCANO #1, Andagua
Valley, 1989.

MOUTH OF THE VOLCANO #2, Andagua
Valley, 1989.

SOUTH COAST

By John Hyslop

The south coast of Peru extends some three hundred miles from Lima along a narrow band traversed by the Pan American Highway. It is overlooked by the pale-blue outline of the towering Andes Mountains, nearly obscured in a haze of heat to the east, and bordered by immense white-sand beaches swept by brisk Pacific Ocean breezes from the west. As the highway stretches its way south, leaving the gray and dismal skies of the capital for the brilliant sunlight that sears much of its length, sometimes, here and there, it skirts the bare traces of the great Inka coastal road, its predecessor by half a millennium and a lonely reminder that the past is ever present on the modern landscape.

The sprawling outskirts of Lima encroach upon seemingly inhospitable desert. Ever increasing in size and number, the *pueblos jovenes*, or "young towns," fill with émigrés from the highlands. Fragmentary cane and wood shelters are thrown up overnight, forming instant slums, and sometime, maybe in a few years, there will be electricity, plumbing, and water, and the first solid foundations of a permanent settlement.

Broad stretches of lunarlike desert landscapes alternate with agricultural valleys fed by small, slow-moving rivers. Remnants of long-abandoned commercial and residential ventures poke out of the sand as poignant monuments of unrealistic dreams. Pristine stretches of desert are interrupted only by occasional gouging cement works and chicken farms, and by road signs announcing Inca Cola and other quaffable liquids to entice truck drivers and motorists to quench their thirst at the next roadside stand. Wind-carved dunes and pebble-covered flats and low hills give way to patches of lush fields and small population centers on stretches of sand-swept highway. Here, also, walled residences and industrial installations mingle with prehistoric pyramids. It is in this un-

questionably bleak environment that the earth shelters some of Peru's richest ancient history.

A widely held coastal legend told that the god Pachacamac capriciously created the first people on earth. A vengeful, destructive deity, Pachacamac ultimately submerged itself in the Pacific Ocean. On adjacent ground, ancient people built a settlement called Pachacamac that survived for nearly 1,500 years and developed into a major political and religious center. For centuries it was the seat of a powerful oracle.

Located a short drive south from Lima, Pachacamac is now a major tourist attraction. Its cemeteries, some of the richest on the coast, have been looted by generations of *waqueros* (treasure hunters). In the last decades a modern town has encroached on Pachacamac, but it remains one of the most important archaeological sites in the Andes.

At the turn of the century, the German archaeologist Max Uhle

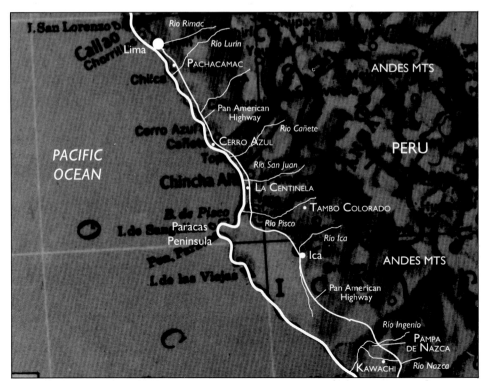

(Left) Cerro Azul, Cañete Valley, 1988. A lighthouse now stands adjacent to the remains of the ancient Inka settlement of Cerro Azul at the sea's edge of the valley. Nearby are the remains of more than twelve truncated adobe pyramids built by the local inhabitants before the Inka conquest of the south coast in the 15th century.

Power poles, pueblo joven, north of Pachacamac, 1989.

carried out the first extensive research on Peru's south coast. At Pachacamac, and in the area to the south, Uhle undertook the archaeological research that began to define the long sequence of diverse Andean civilizations.

One of his discoveries was that the south coast had undergone a period of massive development in the several hundred years before the Inka Empire arrived there in the mid-fifteenth century. Great sites such as La Centinela in the Chincha Valley were built at that time. Its multiple pyramidal-platform structures still rise, visible for miles, over the valley floor.

The Inkas integrated the south coast into their Empire. Their imprint on the area was profound as they remodeled and constructed additions to great centers such as Pachacamac, La Centinela, and Cerro Azul. The latter, a very large pre-Inka site comprising some twelve truncated pyramids, lies just to the south of a once-spectacular Inka fortress, systematically destroyed over the centuries.

Uhle excavated in several valleys, but did not discover some of their inhabitants' most remarkable achievements. Several decades later, on the remote, windswept Paracas peninsula, hundreds of mummies were found with some of the most exquisite ancient textiles known anywhere to archaeologists. The finds at Paracas, dating back more than two millennia, were but one of the region's slowly revealed treasures. Another, so unique that nothing else in the world is quite like it, is found on the desert of Nazca.[1]

NAZCA LINES—DISCOVERY AND EARLY EXPLANATION

In the late 1920s the Peruvian archaeologist Toribio Majía Xesspe observed a variety of unusual markings—lines and paths—on the deserts of Nazca, which, in his published notes some thirteen years later, he suggested were ancient ceremonial or religious roads. His cursory observations, however, did not awaken the curiosity of an international community of scholars. This disinterest would change significantly following the investigations of the American geographer Paul Kosok in the 1940s.

Kosok used aerial photographs to evaluate the geoglyphs (the name by which the figures and lines are known to scientists), and was the first to understand what many others had failed to grasp—that the desert, a region of more than eighty-five square miles, was filled with prehistoric geoglyphs.

Kosok was quick to provide an interpretation for the Nazca lines. Finding that a number of them pointed to solstice positions and to the Pleiades, he pronounced the Nazca lines the "largest astronomy book in the world," thus initiating the explanation

Tambo Colorado, 1989. An Inka administrative center in the Pisco Valley, Tambo Colorado is one of the best-preserved Inka sites in coastal Peru. It was probably built by Emperor Thopa Inka (ca. 1471–1493) following his conquest of southern Peru.

---

[1]Throughout this text, Nazca (with the z) refers to the geographical area and river. Nasca (with the s) refers to the culture. When referring in a general sense to the lines on the pampa, I use "Nazca" since many of the lines may not be of the Nasca culture.

Dog, mercado, Lima, 1989.

that held sway for more than a generation, that the lines were primarily for astronomical and calendrical observations. This theory was propagated by Kosok's protégée, the mathematician Maria Reiche. Needless to say, neither Kosok nor Reiche ever published a convincing set of data proving the astronomical nature of the lines. Indeed, a few lines did point to astronomical events, but given the hundreds of lines it would have been unusual if this were not the case.

Other theories, several approaching the ridiculous, were advanced. One best-seller insisted that the lines were landing fields for spaceships. Another suggested that they were ancient make-work projects for using surplus human resources. Such speculations were made with closed eyes.

From the air, the mind certainly cries out to know the meaning of the bewildering array of "lines" and other designs that form such extraordinary desert patterns. Indeed, the Nazca phenomenon has been, and to some degree remains, one of archaeology's most baffling mysteries. On the other hand, much has been learned, and this information must be taken into account in order not merely to fantasize explanations.

THE GEOGLYPHS—LOCATION, TECHNOLOGY, AND DATE

The greatest concentration of geoglyphs is found on the desert plain (pampa) between the Ingenio and Nazca rivers about 250 miles south of Lima. Numerous others also are found on valley slopes descending to the rivers. Construction of nearly all the lines and figures involved a relatively simple procedure. Dark-colored rocks were removed from the surface, exposing the light sand beneath, with a dark border usually created where stones were deposited on the edge of the figure or line.

A number of geoglyphs abandoned during the process of construction have been discovered. Rocks appear to have been picked up and deposited in sequences of piles before being placed on the outlines. Relatively little labor was required to make even the largest figures. Equally, advanced skills were not necessary. Using ground sighting only, a limited group effort easily could have created a line or figure that was spectacular in size.

Since wind and water erosion on the pampa is minimal, and the surface is nearly free of blown sand and shifting dunes, many of the lines constructed one or two thousand years ago remain visibly etched on the desert floor. Unfortunately, recent human erosion from motorists has done considerable damage. Thanks in great part to Maria Reiche, who, broom in hand, literally chased vehicles off the pampa, the region was saved from greater destruction. Part of it is now protected by security guards—a direct result of Reiche's preservation efforts.

It is widely accepted that the people who made the geoglyphs probably lived on the edges of the irrigated Ingenio and Nazca valleys during the period attributed to the Nasca culture (200 B.C. to around A.D. 600). This highly creative culture produced some of South America's most spectacular textiles and polychrome pottery, but since substantial remains are found in only some five valleys, it does not appear that they dominated a large region.

In the Nazca drainage is the principal ceremonial center, Kawachi, an especially impressive set of platform structures and enclosures whose present eroded and windblown surfaces cause it to blend almost totally with the desert terrain when viewed from the ground. The area around Kawachi and other Nasca sites is scarred by thousands of pits. Each is a looted grave—testimony to the unpardonable destructive effects of illegal commerce in pre-Columbian antiquities.

Carbon dates on wood posts at "line" intersections on the pampa, as well as Nasca ceramic fragments found on the lines and designs on pottery similar to desert motifs, argue that the Nasca culture was responsible for most of the geoglyphs. Other geoglyphs, however, although far fewer in number, are found on the deserts of South America's Pacific coast from the Santa Valley in northern Peru to the Atacama region in Chile. Some ground figures, such as those made by the Paracas culture, predate the Nasca

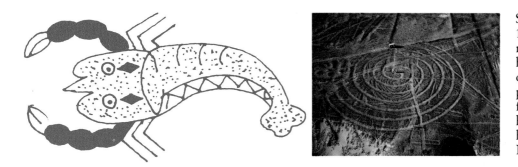

Spiral with van, Nazca, 1987. Spirals may represent rivers or lightning and could have been used in water cults or served as sacred pathways. Over 100 spiral figures, often several hundred feet in diameter, have been recorded at Nazca.

creations. It is also believed now that lines and figures were made in the centuries following the Nasca culture. One survey suggests that most of the linear geoglyphs are post-Nasca. Nevertheless, just how many were late arrivals is still being debated.

The crosscutting, superimposed nature of many of the lines and geometrical features etched so diligently into the desert floor at Nazca can be compared to a giant scratch pad with sets of doodles on top of one another. But one can be certain that the peoples of Nazca were far more serious about their undertaking than a doodler with a pad of paper. The filled scratch pad, of course, is not one preconceived concept but many superimposed ideas. Similarly, lines and figures (as we now see them) were created at different times, many covering and passing over earlier figures. In other words, the markings of Nasca are the results of many generations of line builders. They are not one great enterprise built in a short time from a central plan.

Two general categories of markings on the Nazca desert deserve elaboration. The first are the life-figures (biomorphs), plants, animals, humans, and, possibly, supernatural beings, which are the best known although the fewest in number. The second is the far larger category of lines and geometric figures.

PLANTS AND ANIMALS

There are fewer than fifty biomorphs, almost all located on not more than 5 percent of the pampa on the south side of the Ingenio River. Magnificent from an aerial perspective, most are less than 300 feet in size and usually are dwarfed by longer lines and larger geometric figures. The biomorphs probably were some of the first markings fabricated, and almost all are crossed by lines and geometric figures constructed after them.

What do we know about the biomorphs? First, many imitate life-forms, such as spiders, monkeys, birds, and killer whales painted on Nasca pottery. Their meaning, however, may be debated. The anthropologist Johan Reinhard, drawing evidence from recent Andean ethnographic studies and historical sources

from the last few hundred years, argues forcefully that the biomorphs are all related to a water/mountain/fertility cult. But did the images mean the same more than 1,500 years ago when they were made? Reinhard argues that the meanings of the figures may have remained unchanged during the centuries.

One notable feature of the biomorphs is their construction by a line that never crosses itself. This suggests that they may have been made to be walked upon, since no internal features would impede, symbolically or otherwise, the individual or collective movement of people completing the outline. The figures could have been sensed, in an elated state, by individuals taking part in various "walking" rites. But this is pure speculation. We may never know their purpose, nor what the participants felt who traced their way around the figures.

The ancient makers of the biomorphs certainly lacked the ability to fly and could not have observed them from the air. But the impression that they must have been visualized from on high is hard to overcome, even for hardened scientists who prefer to view the figures terrestrially. One clearly speculative, but plausible, argument for the vertical viewpoint is that the figures were conceived and constructed to be viewed by the floating "winged" creatures that early south-coast people depicted with great frequency on their textiles. Thus, one cannot rule out the suggestion that a true vertical perspective, accessible only to sacred entities, was employed in the design of the biomorphs.

LINES AND GEOMETRIC GEOGLYPHS

Lines and geometrical figures comprise the great mass of markings on the Nazca desert.[2] Lines are long, cleared spaces with borders, and most are quite narrow—no more than half a yard wide. The majority are less than a mile long, although a few reach nearly five miles in length. One of the lines' notable characteristics is their exceptional straightness, often crossing streambeds and

[2]The word "lines," although descriptively inaccurate, is so thoroughly entrenched in the archaeological and popular literature about Nazca that the term will be used in this text.

hills to maintain their course. Many cross over other lines, biomorphs, and geometric figures. In all, more than 620 miles of lines have been traced on the pampa, and wind and water erosion may have obliterated an equal number.

In addition to the lines, there are several types of geometrical features, the most common being large cleared spaces in the form of trapezoids, triangles, and rectangles, with widths ranging from 5 to about 200 yards. A typical trapezoidal figure might measure 36 by 360 yards. Others are much smaller and some considerably larger. The biggest covers 186,567 square yards!

During the early 1980s, the investigators Anthony Aveni, Tom Zuidema, and Gary Urton carried out several years of fieldwork and research at Nazca. Their discoveries give us a revolutionary

Paredones, Nazca, 1988. Paredones, the Inka administrative center that controlled the Nazca region from the mid-15th century, lies beneath a hill etched with modern political graffiti, at the southern edge of the Nazca valley.

view of the Nazca lines that will be fundamental to all future interpretations.

Early maps of the pampa revealed a number of points at which some of the lines converged. Called "star-like centers" by early investigators, they were not viewed as particularly important, nor was it thought that there were many of them. The recent intensive fieldwork has found at least sixty-two line or ray centers on the pampa, most concentrated on or near the edges of elevated plain on the river valleys or on low protrusions that extend into the pampa from mountains to the east. Now known as "line centers," they consist of one or several natural hills topped with one or more piles of boulders. Typically, between ten and twenty lines of diverse widths emanate from them.

The researcher Anthony Aveni reports the astounding observation that, with few exceptions, all of the more than 750 traceable lines on the pampa connect to line centers. Moreover, most of the line centers have one or a number of lines that connect to other centers. Thus radial sets of lines cross and interlace over the entire surface of the desert, making the line centers *the primary class of figure laid down by the ancient peoples of Nazca.* Most geoglyphs are thus sets of radial phenomena and not just a mass of lines and geometrical figures. Indeed, the spoked patterns of the lines require that all explanations address their fundamental radial nature.

Trapezoidal and triangular features are tied into the phenomena of the line centers, since lines emanating from the latter may connect with the larger figures. Similarly, the rarer zigzags of single and parallel lines also emanate from, and sometimes return to, line centers.

Where do the lines go? In many cases erosion on the pampa makes it impossible to know. When lines are fully traceable, a few terminate in dry gulches or a major river. Others end at no specific feature, while still others lead to large geometrical spaces. Finally, some lead to other line centers. This perplexing array of "terminations" is not easily explained and is one of the many

puzzles that remain to confound future investigators. One speculative view is that the lines terminate at the centers and were not intended to originate there.

INTERPRETATION

The idea that lines were used primarily for astronomical observations has not fared well. The hypothesis has now been tested with varied research strategies by several archaeoastronomers, including Gerald Hawkins in the late 1960s and, more recently, Anthony Aveni. Although Aveni's approach was more comprehensive and elaborate than Hawkins' and incorporated known Andean astronomical concepts, he concluded, as did Hawkins, that there was little evidence that the Nazca lines as a whole were a giant calendar or observatory.

The door remains open to the theory that a small number of the lines could have been used for observations, but, as Aveni concludes, astronomical planning was not a general part of the design and layout of all line centers.

There is now general agreement that the lines and figures at Nazca were walked upon or moved over by people. For example, many of the lines have pathways of disturbed sand within them that demonstrate that people traversed them. The lines also have characteristics in common with other ancient desert roads that have cleared beds with stone-lined borders. Stone piles, or cairns, are found on many ancient roads where they change their form or width and where rituals were carried out. Similar cairns are found on some Nazca lines where they cross or change their shape. The straightness of Nazca lines also suggests they were walked upon, since straight routes, often oblivious to topographic obstacles, were and remain important in Andean ritual processions.

The anthropologist Gary Urton has devised a model proposing how the lines may have been used. While he does not suggest the goals of the ceremonies or rituals, he proposes that work groups represented by nearby *ayllu* (Andean kin groups) were responsible for various lines or segments, maintaining them, as Andean people have traditionally accomplished most communal tasks, by a rotational labor system. Thus different groups were responsible for specific lines or figures, periodically sweeping them clean or building new ones. Urton proposes that a dual division (moiety), basic in Andean social structure, existed between groups in the Ingenio Valley and those in the Nazca drainage. The peoples on the northern and southern side of the pampa may thus have created and maintained their figures with a spirit of confrontation and cooperation that so often accompanies tasks accomplished by dual Andean groups and their subdivisions, the *ayllu*.

Urton's explanation, modeled on widespread Andean cultural practices, remains somewhat hypothetical, but it fits well with

Pueblos jovenes, south of Lima, 1989.

(Right) Boys flying kite, El Salvador, south of Lima, 1989. (Far right) Profile of hummingbird, Nazca, 1987. This figure often depicted on early Nasca ceramics measures several hundred feet from beak to tail.

anthropological knowledge about how Andean people organize themselves and accomplish tasks. Certainly, for their builders and users the primary impact of these figures came not from looking at them but from making them, maintaining them, and executing periodic ceremonies on them.

What sorts of rituals were performed on the lines? Much ancient and modern Andean religion concerns water, the all-important commodity necessary for fertility and agricultural production. Any exploration into ancient ritual systems must examine the possibility of water rites. As noted above, many of the line centers are located on the elevated edges of the two rivers that border the pampa. A relationship to water is also suggested by trapezoidal geoglyphs (on the slopes below the pampa of the Ingenio Valley), which have their wider, lower ends pointing to the irrigated land and river. The alignment of some trapezoids parallel to the direction of water flows that run across the pampa during rare rainfalls may also hint at special water concerns.

One Andean ritual system provides many clues for understanding the Nazca line centers. It is the great *zeque* system of Cuzco. Fortunately, a seventeenth-century document describes the system in considerable detail, and it has been studied thoroughly by Tom Zuidema and his colleagues. Forty-one generally straight lines (*zeque*) radiated out, from the capital's Sun Temple. On those lines, some of which were walked upon, there was a set of 328 sacred points (*waqa*). The system integrated and coordinated many elements of Inka thought relating to cosmology, kinship, social hierarchy, ancestors, astronomy, irrigation, natural phenomena, and state ideology.

At Cuzco, members of royal and nonroyal groups performed rituals and made offerings at the *waqa* on the *zeque* lines throughout the year. Those points were often water sources (canals, springs, rivers) or rocks symbolizing many ideas. Other *waqa* were used for cosmological observations, mountain worship, recalling miraculous events, ancestor veneration, the protection of leaders, ensuring a safe journey, and so forth. If one can say any-

thing about the *zeque* system, it clearly was not simple.

The radial centers of Nazca may have been earlier formulations, or predecessors, of the Inka *zeque* system. Indeed, the tentative evidence that some of the line centers may have been made shortly before Inka times indicates a direct passage of the radial ritual system concept from earlier peoples to the Inkas. If such was the case, we are warned by the analogy with Cuzco's *zeque* system, with its demonstrated complexity, that there was probably nothing simple about the configurations in the desert of Nazca. No single-cause explanation will suffice to explain the entire phenomenon. And there may be many important ideas that were expressed on the Nazca pampa that, because of their symbolic nature, will never be defined. A concern with water, mountains, and even astronomy may all be there. But at Nazca there were doubtless many other beliefs and ideas that were dealt with as people moved, worked, or even danced in periodic rituals along the lines and figures.

We can now be quite certain of one thing—that the monumental designs at Nazca are one of the most unique and exquisite expressions anywhere of ancient peoples sanctifying their landscape. For those who love mystery, much of it remains at Nazca.

Aveni, Anthony. "I. An Assessment of Previous Studies of the Nazca Geoglyphs," *The Lines of Nazca*, ed. Anthony Aveni, pp. 1–40, American Philosophical Society, Philadelphia, 1990.

———. "II. Order in the Nazca Lines," ibid., pp. 41–113.

Kosok, Paul. *Life, Land and Water in Ancient Peru*, Long Island University Press, New York, 1965.

Morrison, T. *Pathways to the Gods*, Harper & Row, New York, 1978.

Reinhard, Johan. *The Nazca Lines—A New Perspective on their Origin and Meaning*, Editorial Los Pinos, Lima, 1988.

Silverman, Helaine. "Beyond the Pampa: the Geoglyphs in the Valleys of Nazca," *National Geographic Research*, 6(4): 435–456, Washington, D.C., 1990.

Urton, Gary. "IV. Andean Social Organization and the Maintenance of the Nazca Lines," *The Lines of Nazca*, ed. Anthony Aveni, pp. 174–206, American Philosophical Society, Philadelphia, 1990.

Zuidema, R. Tom. *The Ceque System of Cuzco*, International Archives of Ethnography, Supplement to vol. 50, Leiden, 1964.

Author's Note: The text on the South Coast owes a special debt to Anthony Aveni and Gary Urton, who generously supplied the author with manuscripts on the Nazca lines. Their contributions have been fundamental in the preparation of this essay.

CARHUA, 1989. Ancient house remains, riddled with looters' pits, lie just south of the Paracas peninsula. Following intensive looting in the 1970s, fragments of painted cloth appeared on the international art market, revealing an iconography featuring felines and staff gods that establishes close links to the Chavín cult centered hundreds of miles to the north.

CANDELABRA, Paracas, 1989. This 600-foot-high
trident overlooks the Bay of Paracas. Three-foot
trenches dug into sand outline the 200-foot-wide
figure, known locally as the "Candelabra." Its date and
function remain a mystery. It may have been built
during the colonial period as a beacon to signal Spanish
sailing ships entering the sheltered bay.

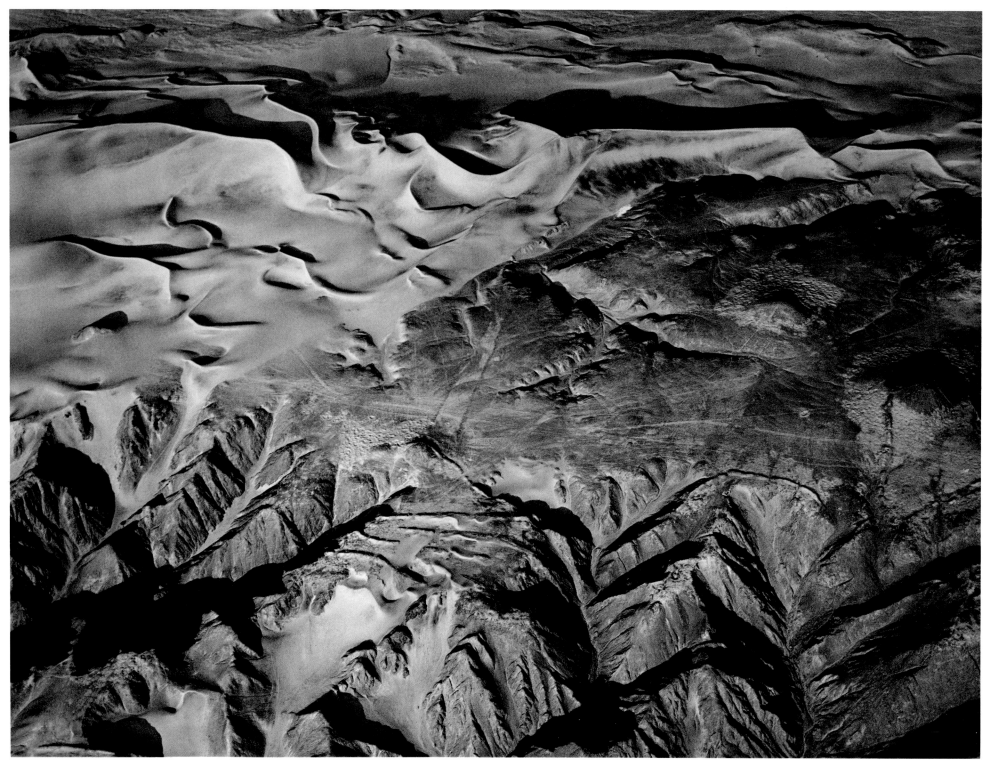

ANCIENT ARROW, south of Ica, 1989. This
weathered trapezoidal figure on a hilltop is one of a
small number of such figures found beyond the Nazca
heartland, many miles to the south. Unlike many of the
Nazca trapezoids, this one points west toward the
ocean.

SAND DUNES AND TRUCK ON COASTAL
PAN AMERICAN HIGHWAY, near Chala, 1989.

PACHACAMAC, 1988. Shantytowns border buildings on the edge of this ancient pilgrimage center. Pachacamac was the most venerated shrine in coastal Peru; its fame preceded by some 500 years its occupation by the Inkas around A.D. 1470. Although the Inkas built a sun temple on the site, they allowed Pachacamac's oracle to continue. Ancient Peruvians believed that Pachacamac, a creator/earthquake god (literally "earth-shaker" in Quechua), punished those who neglected the cult by sending earthquakes. So renowned was Pachacamac's wealth and fame that Spanish conquistador Francisco Pizarro sent his brother Hernando to plunder the site.

TRAPEZOID OVER HILL, Nazca, 1987. A large
cleared trapezoid several hundred feet long lies
alongside low-lying hills bordering the Nazca plateau.

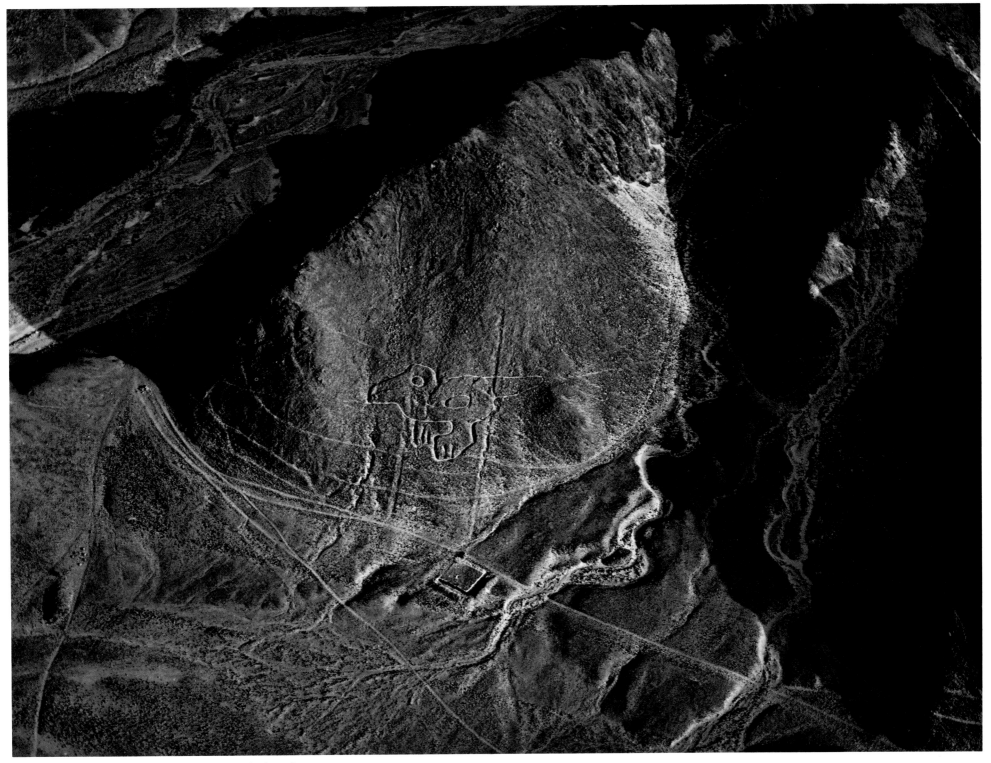

DUCK, Nazca, 1987. Birds represent the majority of some fifty biomorphs represented on the Nazca pampa. Unlike most of the figures, this bird, approximately 100 feet in length, has not been constructed by one continuous line (eye and wing segment) and may be an early rendition, perhaps dating from 500 to 200 B.C.

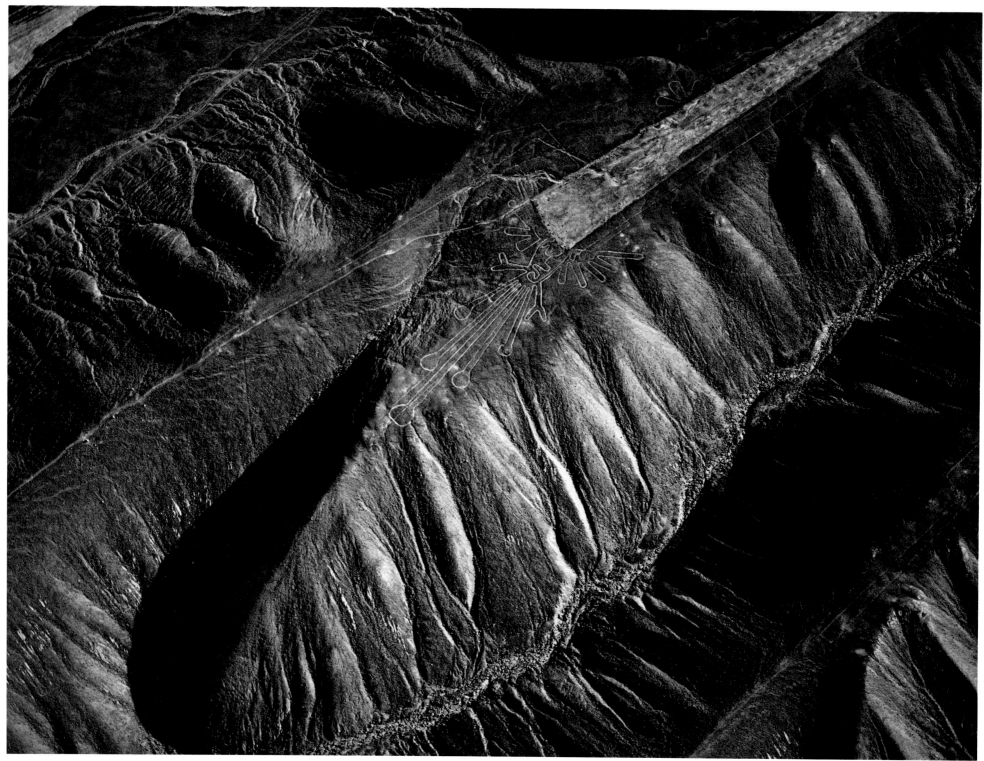

TAIL FEATHERS ON PLATEAU, Nazca, 1988.
The tail feathers and partial trunk of a bird are all that
remain of this figure, which is nearly obliterated by an
immense trapezoid. Sited on a plateau overlooking the
Palpa Valley, north of Nazca's Pampa de San Jose, the
bird's tail arrangements are 160 feet long and 80 feet
wide at their broadest point.

RAY CENTER AMONG LINES, Nazca, 1988. Ray
centers, now considered to be one of the most
important features of the Nazca line system, are small
hillocks at which lines emanate or converge (there is
some controversy on this point) and connect to other
lines, geometric figures, and, in some cases, to other
ray centers. Some sixty-two have been counted.

PATHWAY TO INFINITY, HIGH OVERVIEW, Nazca, 1988. "False trapezoidal" figures are commonplace at Nazca. Instead of the ground covering inside the figure being removed, two cleared lines appear to converge to form a trapezoid; in fact, the lines extend for miles until they are lost in the foothills of the Andes.

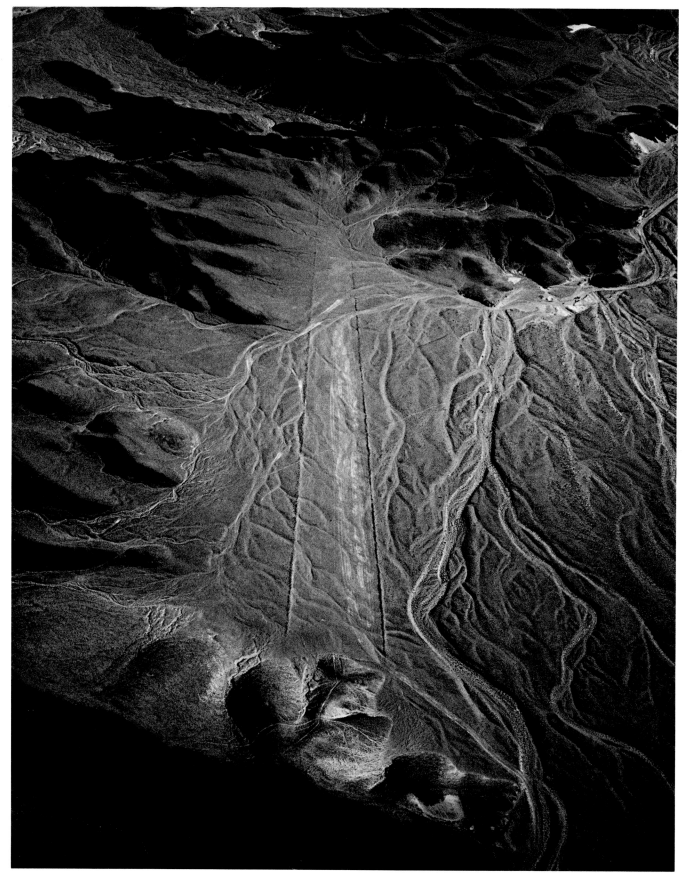

RAY CENTER, Nazca, 1988. More than 750 lines on the pampa connect to ray centers, which were also pivotal points for the construction of numerous broad avenues. There is evidence that maintenance and perhaps "ownership" of various lines and figures were associated with kinship relationships. Deep gullies etched into the desert surface are the result of infrequent rains that inundate the region.

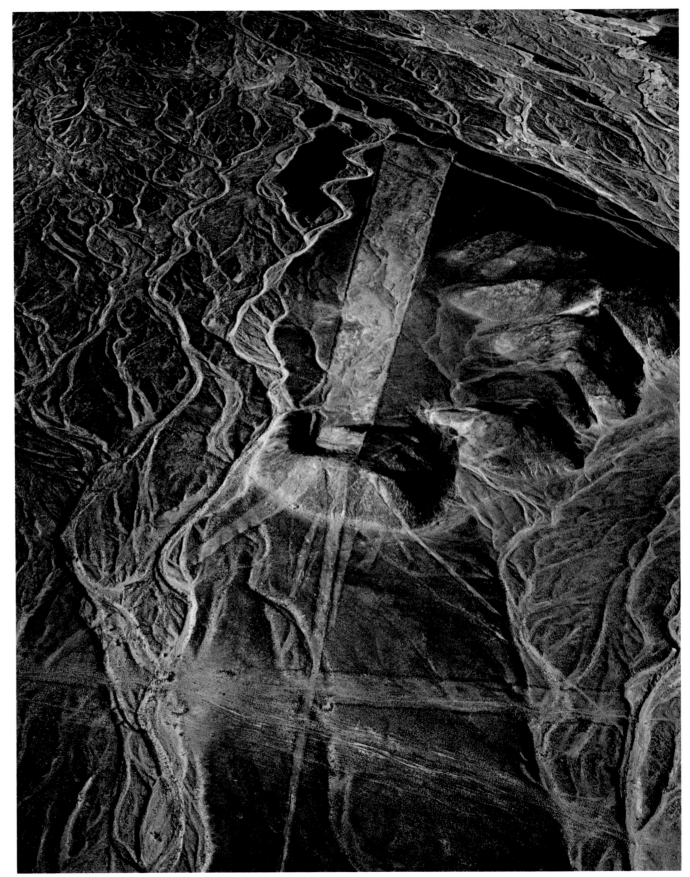

APRA AND ARROWS, Nazca, 1989. On the side of this plateau amid rugged terrain, political graffiti will perhaps become the geoglyphs of tomorrow. The plateau itself is a scratch pad of trapezoids, connecting lines, a ray center (center left), and a fish figure approximately 150 feet long that lies just above the trapezoidal base (left).

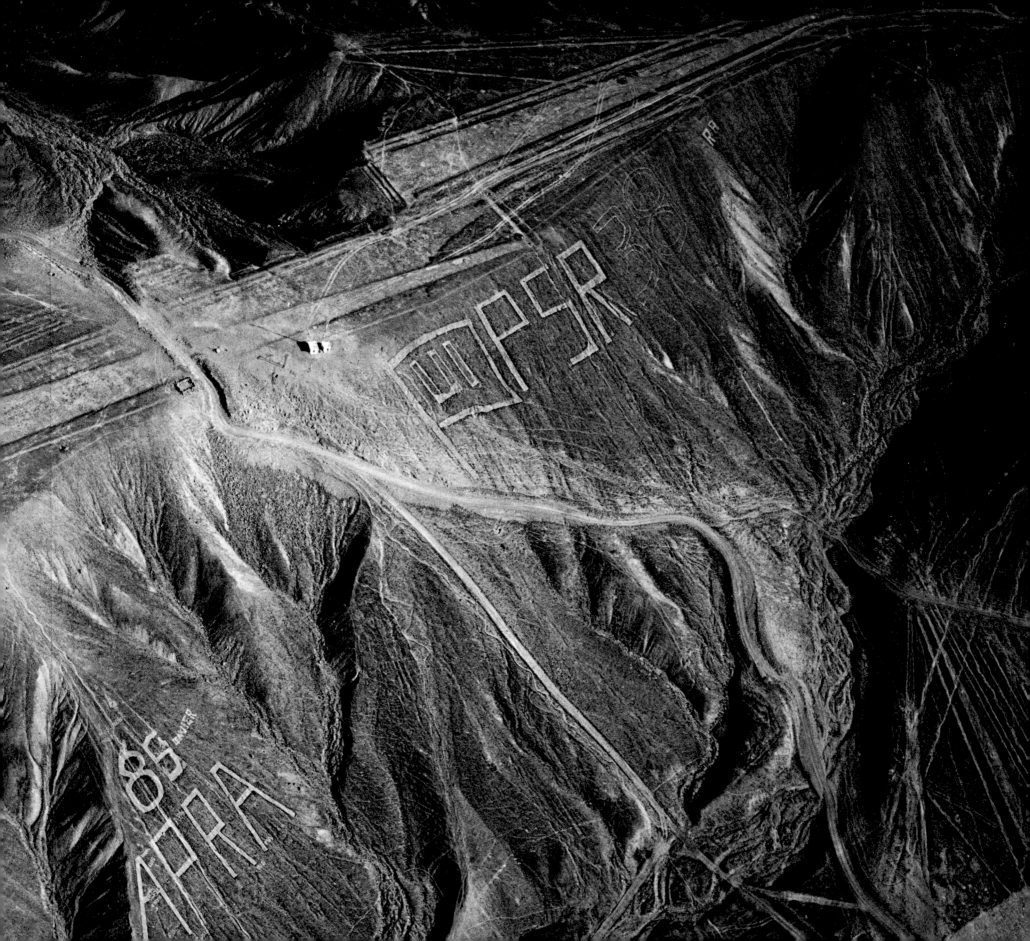

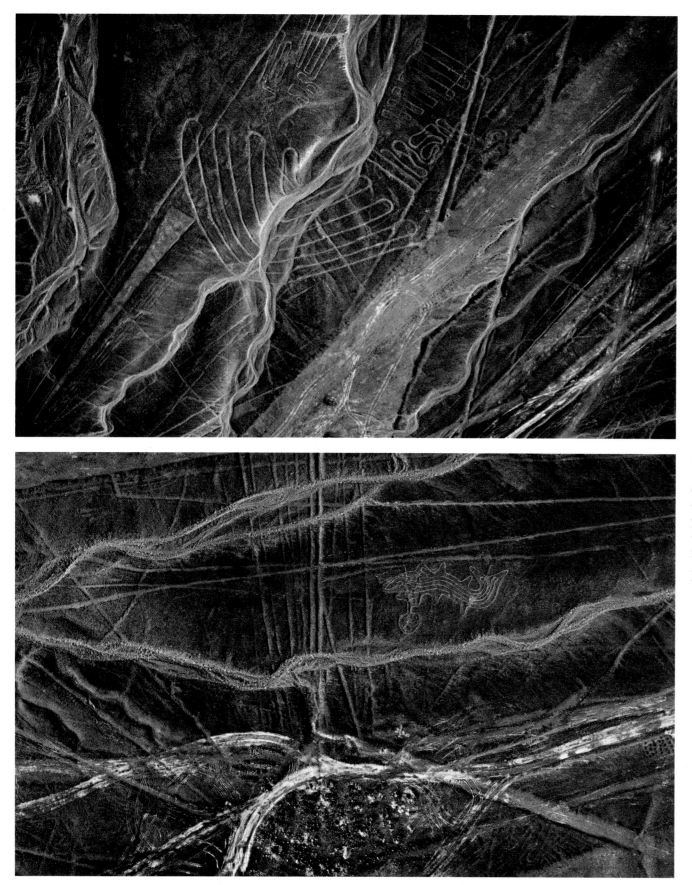

FEATHERS ON PAMPA, Nazca, 1988. A featherlike maze, associated with geometric zigzags, trapezoids, and straight lines, lies on a hilltop north of the Nazca plateau. The profile of a 130-foot marine bird (top, center left) abuts a meandering gully.

KILLER WHALE AND RAY CENTER, Nazca, 1988. Killer whales are often depicted on early Nasca ceramics. This eighty-five-foot figure, perched on the edge of the pampa, overlooking the Ingenio Valley, carries a human trophy head from a lower fin. Trophy-head taking increased in the Nazca region after A.D. 300, and mummified human skulls with ropes have been found in Nasca tombs. The ray center (bottom) has been scarred by unauthorized vehicular traffic.

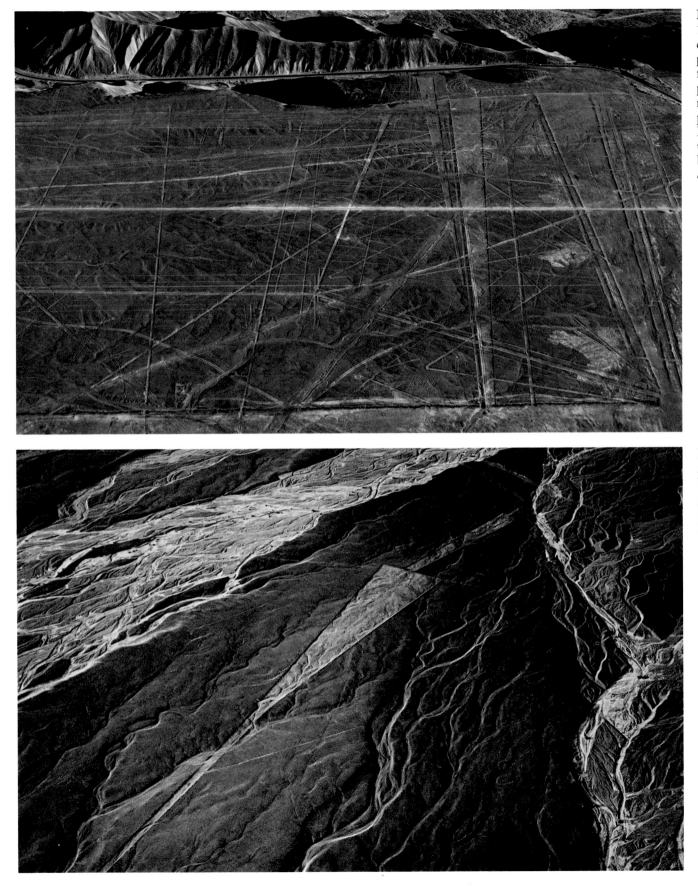

PAMPA ABOVE INGENIO VALLEY, Nazca, 1988. Hundreds of figures, lines, and cleared areas crisscross the desert near Nazca. No single theory can possibly explain the Nazca mystery. The lines and figures may have served several functions: as sacred pathways or to define sacred areas; as astronomical markers; and as reference points for a water cult preoccupied with the veneration of water sources. The Pan American Highway runs left to right at the top of this photograph. The large trapezoid that runs top to bottom (center right), touches a spiral (top) with a diameter of about 260 feet.

INTERSECTING TRAPEZOIDS, Nazca, 1988. About two-thirds of the trapezoid clearings recorded at Nazca have their axes oriented along watercourses. The pointed end usually faces east, or upstream, while the broader base points west, toward the ocean. Here, traces of ancient watercourses border the trapezoid.

LIZARD SPLICED BY PAN AMERICAN HIGHWAY, Nazca, 1988. A truck heads north on the Pan American Highway, which cuts across the pampa and numerous geoglyphs, including a 600-foot lizard (left). The drawing (center) below the highway is a 275-foot representation of a plant, sometimes referred to as seaweed. The observation tower visible below the truck was built by Maria Reiche.

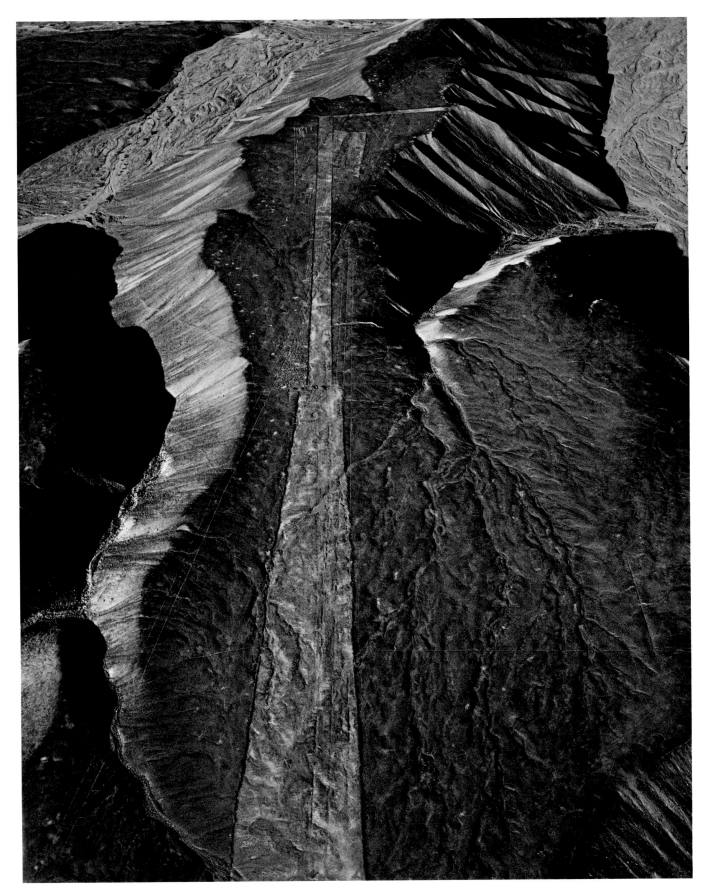

TRAPEZOID WITH EXTENSION, Nazca, 1988. A trapezoidal figure, with connecting trapezoids of diminishing size, follows the course of a plateau near Palpa, north of Nazca. The ancient Nasca people created these giant figures by clearing away darker stones polished by desert varnish from the surface, exposing the lighter-colored sand beneath. Stones were then used to outline the figures.

INCA KOLA, near Lima, 1988. Photographed from
an ultra light aircraft, this storage tank along the Pan
American Highway advertises Inca Kola. No relative
of more famous colas, this drink is yellow in color and
tastes something like a very sweet cream soda.

TOWN OF NAZCA, 1988. Recycling is not a political issue in Peru. Almost everything, including tires, is recycled as a matter of necessity. Until recently, the town of Nazca was a backwater on the Pan American Highway. It now receives hundreds of tourists anxious to view its famous lines from small aircraft.

EXPERIMENT IN DESERT LIVING, Pisco Valley,
1989. Next to these abandoned buildings in the desert
are the faint outlines of prehistoric compounds invisible
on the ground.

HUACACHINA, 1989. The resort of Huacachina
near Ica surrounds an oasis that is one of the few
remaining water holes in this arid coastal valley, where
increasing cultivation of water-intensive crops has
lowered the water table.

MAN ON HIGHWAY, near Lima, 1988.

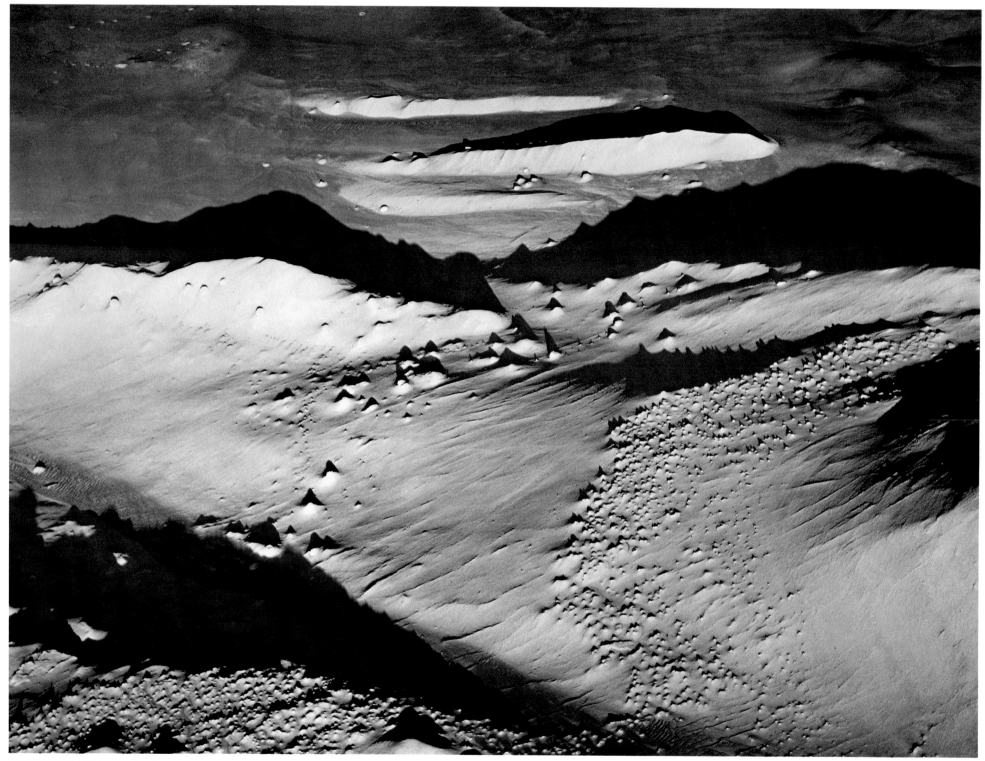

DESERTSCAPE, near Carhua, 1989.

RAY GOD AND CATS, Ica, 1989. Figures on hillsides, such as this human with his headdress and his attendant cats, predate their famous Nazca relatives by several hundred years. They are also smaller. Their ancient builders, probably Paracas-influenced peoples who lived on the coast, created them by heaping stones to trace the outlines of figures.

SEGMENT OF INKA HIGHWAY, near Quebrada de la Vaca, 1989. The Inka road network stretched for more than 14,000 miles, connecting Cuzco, the Inka capital, with the far-flung reaches of the Empire. The Inkas incorporated earlier roads into their system, linking coast, highlands, and jungle via two north-south trunk roads with scores of lateral roads.

POCKMARKS, Pisco Valley, 1989. This 2,600-foot-long chain of stone-lined pits snakes its way up a mountain ridge in the Pisco Valley. This strip of circular pits is nearly forty feet wide, with each pit measuring just over three feet in diameter. Although the function and date of these puzzling pits, unique in Peru, remain unresolved, it has been suggested that they may have served as storage areas for grain.

FIELD SYSTEMS, Atiquipa, 1989. The ancient fields at Atiquipa are still exploited by the region's modern inhabitants, who grow crops sustained by fog-belt precipitation.

KAWACHI, Nazca, 1988. The ancient ceremonial center of Kawachi lies southeast of the modern town of Nazca. Complete with pyramids, plazas, and temples, the Kawachi complex clustered around a natural hill capped by an adobe structure that rose 60 feet above the desert floor. The center lost its prestige after the fall of the early Nasca culture around A.D. 300, although pilgrims continued to visit the site and deposit offerings. The site lies on the southern side of the Pampa de San Jose, and pilgrims may have followed designated lines on the pampa to reach the site. Pockmarks (right and lower right) are looters' pits.

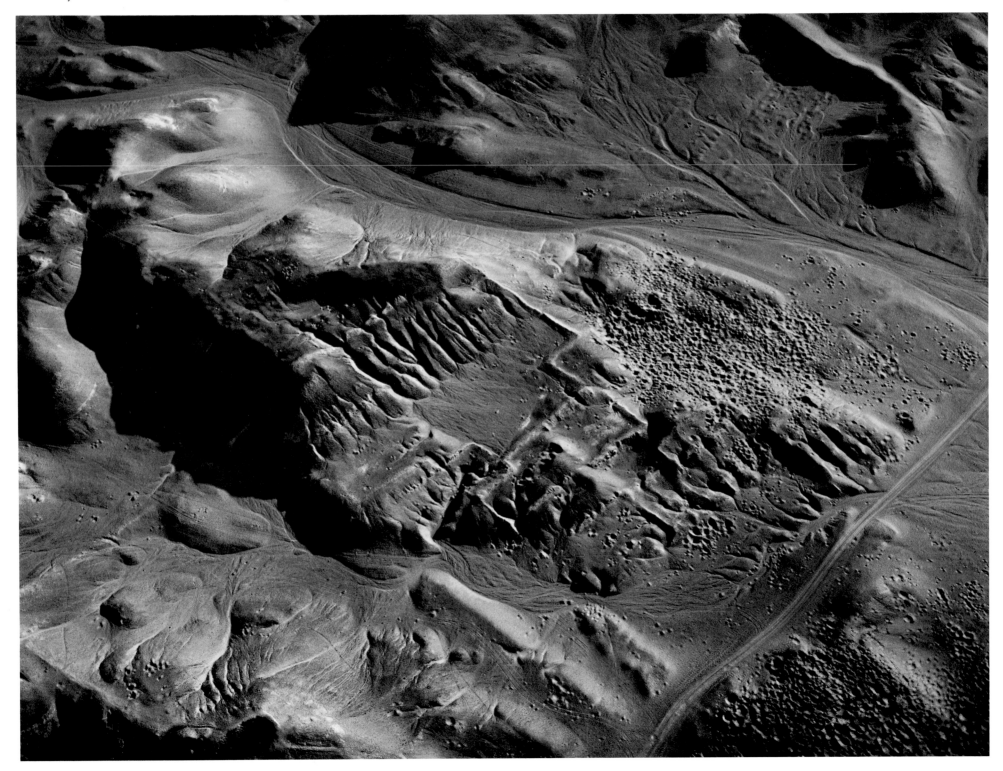

CINDER-BLOCK FACTORY, just south of Lima,
1989.

LA CENTINELA, Chincha Valley, 1989. La Centinela, also known as Tambo de Mora, became the Inka administrative seat in the Chincha Valley after Thopa Inka's armies conquered the area in the 1450s. Pyramids and platform structures, which predate Inka occupation by several hundred years, overlook wide plazas. The lord of Chincha rode in a litter, as did the Inka emperor. He was a casualty at the ill-fated meeting between the Spanish conquistadors and Emperor Atawalpa in Cajamarca in northern Peru in 1532.

NORTH COAST

By John Hyslop

There is no natural demarcation separating the north and south coasts of Peru. Along the entire Pacific littoral, deserts are crosscut by rivers whose waters were the foundation of the agricultural wealth of ancient peoples. From an archaeological perspective, however, the civilizations of the north developed much larger populations and created an abundance of architectural monuments unequaled in the south. In the north, shifting sands shroud extensive ruins while infrequent rainfalls erode pyramids into seemingly natural hills. Hundreds of sites are still unexplored. Judging from the vast amount of architectural remains, the north coast would appear to have been one gigantic megalopolis in preconquest times. We know, of course, that this was not the case. There was not one, but numerous cultures that blossomed and expired over a broad span of time, that left these extraordinary remains.

At the beginning of the second millennium before Christ, the peoples of the north coast were building the largest architectural complexes to be found anywhere in the Americas. The civilizations of the north coast were based on irrigation agriculture supplemented with marine resources. Numerous rivers descend from the Andes to the sea, and for 3,500 years a series of cultures used massive canal-building projects and other irrigation techniques to transform lifeless deserts into the most fertile and abundant region of the Pacific coast.

The north coast covers more than six hundred miles extending from the Lambayeque Valley complex in the north to the Rimac-Chillon complex in the south. At four places the rivers were relatively close together, with no rugged terrain between them. These became the most productive zones of the north, as ancient people linked the rivers with canals, creating vast hydrological systems. The largest of these systems, the Lambayeque complex, joined five rivers and developed into the single most productive area of the Pacific coast.

In the second and first millennia before Christ the monuments of the north coast became increasingly larger, reflecting a growth in the complexity of the social groups that built them. At first the larger settlements were by the sea in the southern part of the north coast, indicating their dependence on marine resources. As time passed, larger settlements were built inland, suggesting a greater reliance on irrigation agriculture. One such site is Cerro Sechín in the Casma Valley. Here, a large enclosure was built with boulders carved with disconcerting figures of intact and dismembered humans. How this puzzling structure fits into the scheme of north-coast chronology is still debated.

Archaeologists have not yet fully defined political units or boundaries for these early times, but periods of peace appear to have been interspersed by warfare between peoples on the coast and in the nearby highlands. Possible evidence for this conflict is the ruins of Chankillo in the Casma Valley. Chankillo appears to be a fortress with three concentric walls and four well-protected

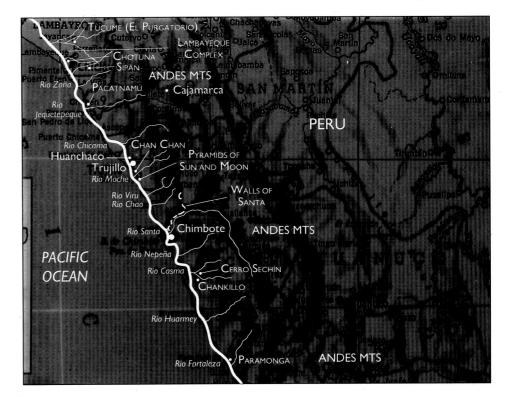

(Left) Factory, Chimbote, 1989.

entrances. The top of the site has two round structures and an enclosure with seven rooms. Never studied in detail, some authorities nevertheless argue that despite its military appearance it is actually a religious complex. Andean peoples have a long tradition of enclosing sacred areas within walls, making it difficult to differentiate forts from temples.

The later centuries of the first millennium before Christ saw the decline or abandonment of some of the well-known centers on the north coast. A new cultural manifestation called Chavín, often thought to be religious in nature and heralding a fierce feline god, spread along the coast, introducing a new art style and new technologies in metalworking, textiles, and ceramics. The causes of the rise and spread of the Chavín cult (which reached as far south as Ica) will be long debated, but its collapse after a few hundred years set the scene for new societies that were fundamentally quite different from their predecessors and whose massive remains would ensure for the north coast of Peru its place among the truly great archaeological zones of the world.

MOCHE

After 100 B.C. most of the larger architectural complexes were constructed on the upper part of the north coast, probably stimulated by irrigation systems that created more arable terrain than was ever accessible on the south. By A.D. 100 the Moche culture coalesced with its nucleus in the Moche Valley, where the modern city of Trujillo is now located. For six hundred years Moche flourished, expanding over 250 miles from the Nepeña Valley in the south to the Lambayeque Valley complex in the north.

Much is known about life in Moche times because sites have been studied extensively by archaeologists and because its extraordinary pottery depicts people engaged in many different activities. Great lords appear richly attired and are often portrayed surrounded by retainers and captives. Important individuals were carried in elegant litters. Complicated hunting scenes painted on pottery depict elaborately dressed hunters capturing deer with

dogs and nets and killing them with clubs or with spears launched from spear throwers. Persons performing menial tasks are often portrayed nude or with loincloths. Manifestations of disease, birth defects, and wounds of war are explicitly depicted. Specialized sexual scenes, many depicting heterosexual anal intercourse and fellatio, are graphically modeled in ceramics. Experts note that the activities are generally nonprocreative.

Despite the abundance of varied and explicit subject matter, however, Moche expert Christopher Donnan points out that scenes of Moche activities must not be interpreted too literally. Many everyday activities are not portrayed, and those that are, such as washing hair, sexual acts, or hunt scenes, really portray religious and symbolic activities. Donnan concludes that Moche

Urban development, Lambayeque Valley, 1988. Available land of any sort is surreptitiously occupied on the outskirts of cities. Here, the higher up the hillock, the least desirable is the real estate, because water has to be hand carried.

(Right) Bird, Chan Chan, 1989. Detail from interior wall. (Far right) Church, Huanchaco, 1989.

art mainly expresses religious and supernatural rites and that there was no attempt to depict daily life for its own sake.

The extraordinary discovery in 1987 of the burial of a Moche lord in a burial platform at Sipán in the Lambayeque Valley brought great media attention to Peruvian north-coast antiquities. The regal individual was buried with retainers and an astounding collection of gold and silver objects. Thereafter, another grave was excavated that exceeded the first in its hoard of gold and silver artifacts and other luxury funerary goods. One fantastic necklace is composed of a series of large gold spiders perched on webs of gold. The Sipán burial platform has already produced the most sumptuous burials ever found by archaeologists in the New World, and more rich graves may still be uncovered.

The Moche constructed their main settlement or capital around the so-called Pyramids of the Sun and the Moon, immense adobe structures in the Moche Valley. The Pyramid of the Sun, the larger of the two facing edifices, reaches 135 feet above ground and covers 12.5 acres. When it was built, it was the largest structure in South America. Approximately 1,000 feet in length, it remains one of the greatest ancient monuments in the New World. Unfortunately, much of the great stepped pyramid has been destroyed by an irrigation channel. It has been estimated that 140 million rectangular adobe bricks were used in its construction.

The Moche people built more modest monuments similar to the pyramidal structures in the Moche Valley in other valleys, particularly to the south. For each valley the installations were usually the largest buildings of their time and appear to be regional administrative centers. This governing network suggests that Moche culture was spread by conquest.

Moche culture to the north of the Moche Valley is less well documented. One great settlement with a late Moche occupation is Pacatnamú on the cliffs above the mouth of the Jequetepeque River. The site is a magnificent array of dozens of platform pyramids and compounds. Unlike many Moche settlements, Pacat-namú was not abandoned with the collapse of its parent culture but continued to be occupied, and even expanded in size, during the centuries that followed.

In the eighth century Moche culture began to fade. Its capital was moved to the north, and the southern frontier contracted. Experts argue the reasons for this decline, but there is evidence that it was precipitated by a series of natural disasters—earthquakes, drought, and climatic changes—that would have affected the irrigation systems catastrophically and severely reduced coastal fishing. By about A.D. 750 the Moche ceased to exist, and a truly golden age of ancient life had closed.

WARI

New types of artifacts and textiles appear on the north coast at about the time of the Moche collapse. They are linked to a culture called Wari, which was based in the central highlands but spread its influence over most of Peru for some two hundred years. Authorities disagree on whether Wari actually controlled the north coast or merely influenced it. Some have suggested that Wari influence may have hastened the collapse of the Moche, while others say it filled a vacuum created by a Moche culture already in decline. Lack of clearly defined north-coast installations with Wari architecture argue that Wari did not control the area. But one might note that the much later Inka occupation of the north coast also left no Inka architectural imprint; thus, the lack of settlements with a Wari design does not rule out Wari political domination and control.

A remarkable monument created during the period of Wari influence (although not Wari in origin) is the so-called "Great Wall of Peru," which is found north of the Santa River Valley. Originally reported as a single construction, it has been described as the longest "defensive wall" in the New World. Recent investigations have shown, however, that it is not a continuous entity but rather seven different segments that were never connected. Together, their length is about forty-six miles. On average, the

Paramonga, 1989. Five terraced walls surround this formidable, shallow-platform structure that caps a hill in the Forteleza Valley north of Lima. Although often referred to as a fortress, it was probably an Inka temple.

walls are nearly three yards high and three yards wide at their base, with sloping sides leading up to a narrow top. They are constructed with a variety of materials, such as adobe bricks and stones.

Given the number of gaps between the segments, some wider than a mile, it is difficult to think the walls served a defensive purpose. It has been suggested that the sections of wall may have served as boundaries between groups or served to control commerce on roads that passed along the coast. The new interpretations are more plausible than the older defensive theory, but the walls of Santa still retain their mystery, awaiting more data that may clarify their role.

LAMBAYEQUE AND CHIMU

Two major cultures, Chimú and Lambayeque, developed after the brief Wari period on the north coast. The Classic Lambayeque culture (ca. A.D. 800 to 1350) dominated the biggest intervalley irrigation system in Peru, and its rulers erected the Batán Grande pyramids, which became a religious and burial center of great significance.

The great power and prestige of the Classic Lambayeque culture is demonstrated by the colossal settlement of Túcume, or El Purgatorio (so named because it is located inland from cool coastal breezes, and daytime temperatures are blistering). More than two dozen gigantic adobe pyramids partially surround a sharp desert peak. They appear older than they are, since infrequent but heavy rains have eroded them disastrously. Túcume seems to have served as the center of the Lambayeque culture when it was conquered by the Chimú state in the fourteenth century. Once confused with Chimú, the Classic Lambayeque culture is now recognized as an independent entity that left remains unrivaled in their monumentality.

To the south, the Chimú state began its ascendancy sometime between A.D. 800 and 1000. The core area of the state was within the region of the old Moche culture, but during the fourteenth century it expanded over the entire north coast from the Peruvian-Ecuadoran border in the north to a southern extreme just north of Lima. The Chimú formed the largest state that ever developed on the coast of Peru. It is famous not only for its size but also because extensive archaeological research and documents from the early Spanish period reveal many fascinating details about it.

The magnificent capital of the Chimú state, Chan Chan, is located in the Moche Valley and has a core area of about 2.3 square miles. Its surrounding buildings scatter over an area three times larger. Chan Chan's population is estimated to have been somewhere between 28,000 and 69,000 people. Outstanding features of the complex are nine great rectangular enclosures two hundred to six hundred yards long. The exterior walls sometimes exceed ten yards in height. The enclosures, called *ciudadelas*, were built by Chimú rulers and were used for royal burials, storage, and the residence of the king and his retainers. The *ciudadelas* include walls with ornate decorations in clay relief. Water was available in each compound from a large sunken garden or well.

Chan Chan was famous for its luxury and pomp. Its lords rode about in spectacularly adorned litters and were brilliantly attired in gold and silver, feathers, and fine textiles. They were buried ceremoniously in great adobe platforms within the compounds, but today's world will never know the doubtlessly splendid details of how a Chimú king was laid to rest. Before modern times, the regal Chimú tombs were thoroughly looted by the Inkas and then the Spanish.

The Chimú administered their domain through a series of settlements located in the valleys they conquered, often utilizing centers that were already established. Thus the Chimú occupied older sites, such as Pacatnamú, that were characterized mainly by large pyramidal platforms rather than the enclosures of Chan Chan. Chimú walled compounds, however, were built on a more modest basis in a few valleys. This is certainly clear evidence that the Chimú proliferated their own architectural style as their state expanded.

INKA

Around A.D. 1470 the Inka Empire conquered the north coast of Peru, and the Chimú king, Minchançaman, was taken as an "honored" hostage to Cuzco, no doubt to ensure the loyalty and passivity of his subjects. The domination of the Chimú was the Inkas' single greatest conquest. Archaeologists have found evidence suggesting that in this period the north coast was undergoing a decline in its population. Possibly the region was not as populous as in earlier times and not as strong militarily.

With time, the Inkas dismantled the power and organization of the great Chimú state, and different valleys or irrigation systems were placed under the control of independent lords, often local royalty, who were directly responsible to Cuzco.

Walls, Chan Chan, 1989. The latticed interior plaza walls of the former Chimú capital were often decorated with friezes featuring birds, fish, and mythical beings.

The Inkas showed great interest in the social institutions, art, and technology of the Chimú and usurped a number of them. Chimú metalworkers and other artisans were sent to work in Cuzco. Plunder from the Chimú region, particularly gold, was brought back to Cuzco. Much of the gold the Spanish seized from the Inkas may have been taken by the Inkas from the Chimú several generations earlier.

The Inkas constructed little on the north coast, probably because a vast system of roads and settlements already existed and there was little need to erect new installations. But one quite unique site, Paramonga, is found in the Forteleza Valley. The first Spaniards to see it thought it was a fortress because of its five high terrace walls perched on a rocky hill. In fact, the complex was probably an Inka temple. The four small rooms on its summit are an unlikely defensive unit. Paramonga's impressive walls were once painted white and red, and it was decorated with adobe friezes and murals.

The building of splendid monuments on the north coast ceased with the Inka period. The Spanish conquest in the 1530s brought disease and depopulation, and political disorder replaced the knowledgeable and systematic native administration. The great irrigation systems fell into disuse, and, only a generation after the beginning of Spanish rule, eyewitnesses reported vast tracts of deserts where once bounteous fields reached as far as the eye could see.

Donnan, Christopher. *Moche Art of Peru*, Museum of Cultural History, University of California, Los Angeles, 1978.

Lumbreras, Luis G. *The Peoples and Cultures of Ancient Peru*, trans. Betty J. Meggers, Smithsonian Institution Press, Washington, D.C., 1974.

Menzel, Dorothy. *The Archaeology of Ancient Peru and the Work of Max Uhle*, R.H. Lowie Museum of Anthropology, University of California, Berkeley, 1977.

Moseley, Michael E. "The Evolution of Andean Civilization," *Ancient Native Americans*, ed. Jessee D. Jennings, pp. 491–541, W.H. Freeman and Co., San Francisco, 1978.

Parsons, Jeffrey R. and Charles M. Hastings. "The Late Intermediate Period," *Peruvian Prehistory*, ed. Richard W. Keatinge, pp. 190–229, Cambridge University Press, Cambridge and New York, 1988.

Wilson, David. *Prehispanic Settlement Patterns in the Lower Santa Valley, Peru*, Smithsonian Institution Press, Washington, D.C., 1988.

CHANKILLO, Casma Valley, 1989. This hilltop
redoubt on the southern side of the valley probably
dates to around 200 B.C. The thick concentric walls,
stairways to tops of walls, and offset entrances are all
highland features and point to increasing contact
between coastal and highland peoples during this time.

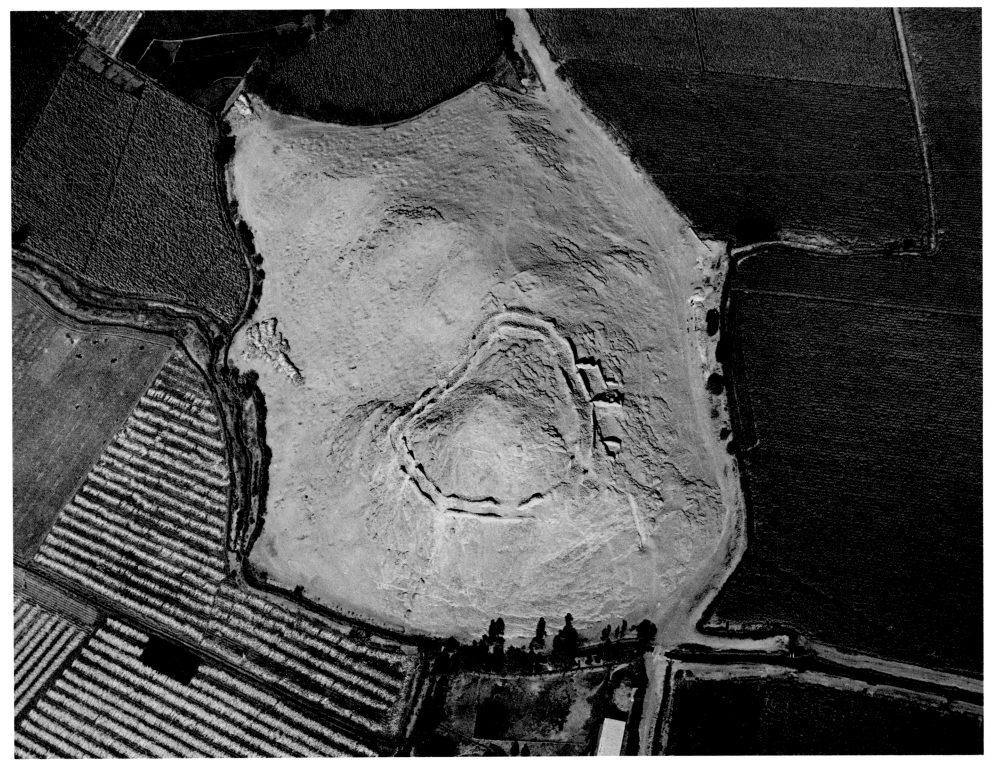

UNIDENTIFIED HILLTOP SITE, Chicama Valley,
1989. Concentric walls are the prominent feature of this
hilltop site, one of many yet to be studied by
archaeologists.

CHOTUNA, Lambayeque Valley, 1988. Due west of
the modern town of Lambayeque, the summit of the
adobe pyramid of Chotuna was reached by a ramp.
Originating in the late Moche period, around A.D.
600, it was occupied through the Chimú period.
Remains of ancient canals near the complex indicate
that its fields were once watered by an irrigation system
that linked three river valleys.

SIPAN, Lambayeque Valley, 1988. Plundered by looters and ravaged by rains, Sipán's two adobe pyramids rise above irrigated fields and loom over a low burial platform (foreground). In 1987, excavators discovered the burial remains of a Moche lord, dating to around A.D. 300, accompanied by retainers and great numbers of gold and silver objects. Since then, another lavish burial has been found.

CHAN CHAN, 1989. The sprawling adobe capital of the Chimú empire, Chan Chan, covers more than six square miles near the modern city of Trujillo. Nine royal compounds and associated structures once housed tens of thousands of people. The exterior adobe walls of the compounds reach thirty feet in height and are up to 600 yards long. The photograph depicts the interior of the Velarde royal compound. The Chimú extended their rule over the north coast from about A.D. 1000 until the Inka conquest around 1470.

ANCIENT RIDGED FIELDS, Casma Valley, 1989.
These fields lie one mile inland from the coast, near the
mouth of the Casma River, and are unique in South
America because they are built on low-lying arid land.
Created by the Chimú between ca. A.D. 1000 and
1470, the field systems were abandoned shortly after
the Spanish conquest in the 1530s.

PACATNAMU AT VALLEY'S EDGE, 1988.
Located at the mouth of the Jequetepeque River,
Pacatnamú is a sprawling complex of more than fifty
adobe temples and associated plazas and covers
approximately one square kilometer. Most of its flat-
topped pyramids date from late Moche (ca. A.D. 600)
and Chimú (ca. A.D. 1000) periods.

ERODED PYRAMIDS, Pacatnamú, 1989. Also called Barranca, Pacatnamú is named after General Pacatnamú, who was sent from Chan Chan by the Grand Chimú, the absolute ruler, to conquer the Jequetepeque Valley and occupy the site. All of the pyramids at Pacatnamú are heavily eroded.

GREAT WALL OF PERU, Santa Valley, 1989. The Great Wall of the Santa Valley rises and dips along ridges near the coastal town of Chimbote. Several different segments, which were never connected, have a combined length of some forty-six miles. The walls are about nine feet in height. Originally thought to be a defense wall, new interpretations suggest it may have served as a boundary marking territorial divisions.

HUANCHACO, 1989. Restaurant by the sea near the ancient fishing village of Huanchaco to the northwest of Chan Chan.

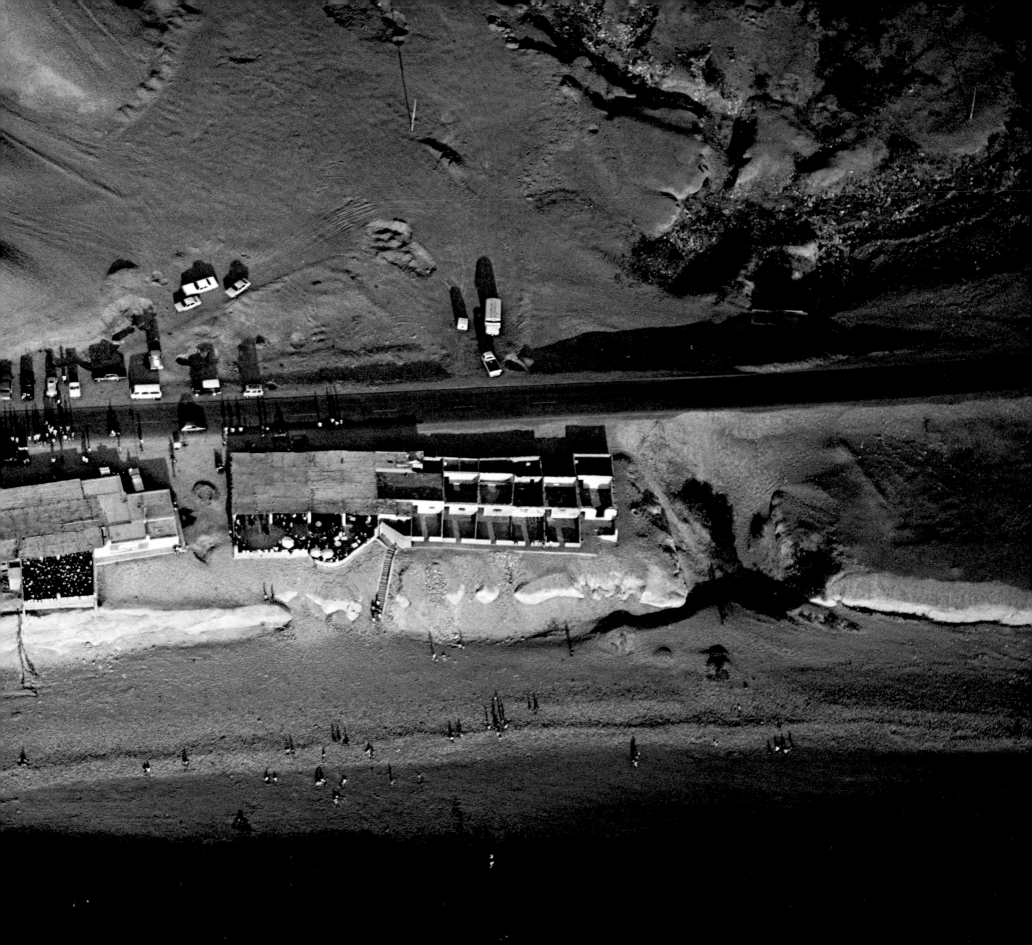

EL PURGATORIO, Lambayeque Valley, 1988. El Purgatorio, or Túcume, is the largest complex of monumental adobe structures in the New World. The site's 26 pyramids surround a low hill and cover some 500 acres. The architects of Túcume incorporated the hill of La Raya into their design, extending the flat-topped Huaca Larga, or Long Pyramid, up to the base of the hill. Main construction dates to around A.D. 1300, although the region was also occupied by Chimú, Inka, and colonial peoples. Pockmarks on the top of the pyramid are the result of digging by looters and infrequent heavy rains.

PYRAMID OF THE MOON, Moche Valley, 1989. Largely unexcavated and overlooking an open area or plaza, the small Pyramid of the Moon faces the much larger Pyramid of the Sun. Both pyramids served as the political center of the Moche kingdom between A.D. 100 and 600.

PYRAMID OF THE SUN, Moche Valley, 1989. An estimated 140 million adobe bricks were used to build the Pyramid of the Sun, or Huaca del Sol, which once stood over 135 feet high and reached 1,000 feet in length. Spanish colonial treasure hunters diverted the waters of the Moche River and eroded away roughly two-thirds of the pyramid.

CERRO SECHIN, Casma Valley, 1989. The central part of the 150-square-foot temple at Cerro Sechín is faced by a stone wall built of more than 400 carved stone slabs portraying a procession of personages and a jumbled array of disarticulated human heads, arms, and legs. The procession may commemorate a victory by highland conquerors over coastal peoples around 1300 B.C.

UNEXPLORED RUINS, Viru Valley, 1989.

AFTERWORD

By Marilyn Bridges

Our plane vibrated threateningly, buffeted by winds churned by the early-morning air of the Andes. Jungle-covered slopes flanked the aircraft, as the pilot almost magically held the plane midway between the valley's sides—mindful that frequent downdrafts could suck us into a mountain if we strayed too far off the median. As a pilot, I was all too aware of the situation. Below, but too close in an aircraft, was the elegant, twisting shape of the Urubamba River, the Great Snake of the Sacred Valley, gateway to Machu Picchu, our destination.

This wouldn't be my first rendezvous with the "Lost City of the Inkas." I had been there by train, among gregarious tourists. I had hiked the weeklong, laborious, and sometimes dangerous "Inka Trail" from Cuzco to reach its great Sun Gate and overlooked its silent majesty blanketed by golden morning sun. And I had flown over it twice before, once hitching a ride in an errant military helicopter, and both times was frustrated by its almost perpetual cloud cover, by mist and rain, even by smoke from jungle slash-and-burn fires, and was unable to photograph it. The morning's weather report in Cuzco, where we took off, was favorable. And so it had been twice before. But this time I knew it would work out. The plane was all wrong. And in the Andes, you learn you can always count on the illogical to triumph.

I had waited three days to find an aircraft to take me to Machu Picchu. I could have waited three weeks. Because of cocaine trafficking, aircraft are scarce, and because of the growing insurgency of the Shining Path guerrillas, now all too close to Cuzco, military restrictions on aircraft made flying almost prohibitive. The plane I hired had just flown in from the jungle. I would have taken anything. It was low-winged, and therefore undesirable for aerial photography, but with desperate persistence I managed to get the pilot to take off the rear cargo door so I could get my shots. Shooting with the door removed from a plane was not a new experience for me, but the pilot was understandably reluctant; the door to his plane had never been removed in flight before,

and he wasn't sure that a plane so light in this condition would be airworthy in the mountains. He was very close to being right. Once aloft, not an easy task with such thin air at a ground-level altitude of eleven thousand feet, the inside of the aircraft mimicked a small cyclone, causing the plane to pitch and making it extremely difficult to maneuver in the narrow valleys we were flying through. The deafening noise also made it virtually impossible for me to communicate with the pilot. I had to move to the front of the plane and shout in his ear to get him to circle or turn one way or another so I could get an oblique or absolute vertical shot. Meanwhile, he was using oxygen to keep his head straight, but none was available for me. Only the cold wind rushing by my face as I lay on the floor of the plane by the open door kept me revived. There were no seat belts to strap me in, so an archaeologist friend who had decided to accompany me was put to work holding my ankles while I shot. The pilot was adamant that he did not want to lose a gringa over the Sacred Valley.

Finally, Machu Picchu was in sight. Nestled between verdant mountain peaks high above the valley floor, the great Inka city-sanctuary is as spectacular today as it must have been four centuries ago when it was accessible only by a precarious trail cut into the mountains. I insisted on circling it numerous times—absorbing its spiritual resonance as much as trying to capture its aura on film. Finally the pilot, fearing that I was experiencing a "state of grandeur" from lack of oxygen, insisted that we pull away. I had obtained my photos. But I also believe that I had come as close as I ever would to flying on the back of a condor.

Peru has always been a magical country for me, and doubly so because it was there that I first photographed from the air. While on an assignment from a travel magazine in 1976, I was coaxed into an aircraft to take photographs of the enormous prehistoric ground drawings on the pampa at Nazca, which can only be seen in their entirety from the air. The flight in a single-engine airplane was a do-or-die initiation. Thermals over the desert rocked the plane constantly, not only scaring me intensely but also making

The photographer stands alongside the *Intiwatana* (hitching post of the Sun) on Machu Picchu, which is a sacred carved Inka boulder where offerings were made.

me rather sick. Despite this negative reinforcement, what I was seeing below me was so fantastic that I was instantly hooked on flying and aerial photography. I've been to Nazca so many times since then, always coming out of the sky, that the locals have nicknamed me "E.T." They wonder why this smiling, tall, blue-eyed woman keeps returning. It's really very simple: I return there as if to an old friend.

Being airborne must be like being reborn. As earthbound creatures, our thought and vision are quite understandably linked to the physical plane, and we ignore or at least minimize transcendental experience. Pilots, astronauts, undersea explorers, even mountain climbers, are fortunate. They must learn to function in alien environments and to experience unique perspectives. Seeing from above is not consistent with seeing from the ground. It is not just a matter of up and down. It took me quite some time to be able to condense information from such a large scale of vision. Seeing from a bird's perspective with very human eyes initially can be confusing—one gets lost in the sweep of imagery and feels restricted by the apparent flatness of everything. But when one flies and photographs, as I do, at low altitudes, shadows lift objects from the ground, and, instead of cold geometric patterns on the earth's surface, intimacy is regained. There is the unmistakable awareness of warmth of contact and a vivid awareness of interrelationships.

I admit to having a strong affinity for the past. Not that I regard the past as perfect and the present as diabolical. But I do believe that in the past man was more in touch with the natural order of the planet; that indigenous peoples regarded their land as a living part of the universe, and that man's tenure on the planet was one that balanced the forces of nature with man's needs. From the air, man's past and his present can be seen in isolation and in conjunction. The former seems coeval with its environment, the latter seems dislocated. Part of my reason for shooting ancient sites is to use imagery to reflect upon the sacred knowledge of the past—truths that remain locked in stone and earth. In my work,

I hope to unlock some of the messages, not through the intellect, where they are undecipherable, but rather through the spirit, where they can be recognized.

Although I had traveled throughout Peru on the ground, except for Nazca I had never shot there from the air. In 1988 I felt a need to do so and applied to the Fulbright Commission for a fellowship to Peru. It was approved, and I left in August for Cuzco, the former Inka capital, which would be my home base.

Cuzco continues to be an Indian city in both population and mystique. Remains of Inka architecture are everywhere, and there is a resonance here, as in all cities, that reflects the collective spirit of the people. Here the resonance is a mournful echo of the past. The present merely sleepwalks in another time.

I taught photography classes at the Cuzco School of Art. These were mostly classes in "seeing," because only three cameras were available for a class of thirty official students and many others would crowd the doorways listening to the lectures. When I was through talking, there would be an explosion of questions. I've never had such an enthusiastic audience. Through their eyes I started to experience more than the surface level of Peru—to see more into the depth of time. Through my eyes I hope they were able to learn how to capture their time as it awakens in the present.

As my experience photographing Machu Picchu suggests, flying and photographing from the air in Peru is no easy task. Not only is there a shortage of aircraft, but it is extremely costly, prohibitive if it weren't for my grant. In addition, shortage of fuel dares one to take unpardonable chances. We often flew with gasoline cans on board. This amounts to knowingly sharing company with a potential bomb. Also adding to normal flying hazards are the growing number of red zones, where planes are subject to ground fire from guerrillas and cocaine traffickers. Most of the pilots I found to fly with were either great pilots or soon-to-be-dead pilots. Even the best pilots number their crashes. Planes are in chronic need of repairs. Some are so patched up that parts become dislodged in flight. You know that things are desperate when you hear of pilots with planes in such bad shape that they purposely crash them so they can collect the insurance money.

The state of the art of flying in Peru came home to me most strongly on one occasion when I hired a pilot to fly me along the coast. Although I am a pilot myself, I always prefer to fly with another pilot when possible so that I can concentrate on photography and he can concentrate on navigation and keeping us airborne. This time the pilot insisted that the mechanic also fly with us. I thought this was for insurance, in case our plane malfunctioned and we had to make an emergency landing in a red zone—the mechanic would be able to fix the plane quickly and we could get to safety. Later I learned that the real reason was to make sure the aircraft was mechanically sound. If the mechanic agreed to come with us, the plane had to be airworthy.

Photographing from the air along the coast has to be confined to a few hours after dawn or just before dusk. Because the landscape is monochromatic, only at these times do shadows delineate subject matter. The whole of Peru's coastline is a sprawling desert interrupted by river valleys of lush green growth. Dunes of fantastic shapes punctuate the blanket of sand, and amid this glaring wasteland ancient cities and sanctuaries make their appearance as sand-laden adobe, abandoned and often undisturbed by modern times. In the population centers of the river valleys, modern architectural forms contrast with ancient ground plans of vast pre-Columbian settlements. Modern city sprawl spreads its tentacles with no visible sense of order; the structures at the extremities are little more than utilitarian boxes amid the discarded refuse of the city proper. In contrast, the ancient structures seem adapted to their environment—comfortable in their space and oriented to natural land forms.

Flying in the highlands is much different than flying on the coast, both visually and in terms of flying experience. Navigational assistance hardly exists when flying anywhere in Peru, so getting lost is a common occurrence. One has to depend on visual sightings or listening to radio stations to establish a fix. Going down (crashing) on the coast is bad enough, but in the mountains there is virtually no chance for survival. There are more stories of more lost planes than anyone wants to hear.

Despite these looming problems, shooting in the Andes is a wonderful experience. Mountain peaks rise from lush jungle growth and shelter valleys with extraordinary agricultural terracing interconnected like a puzzle on the landscape. Along mountain slopes and on small plateaus, ancient ruins are surrounded by small villages where descendents of the Inkas go about their lives only moderately changed from the days when these valleys were the heart of an empire. Here the Inkas built their altars to honor the sun, the glorious deity they could always count on to rejuvenate life. From the air it is easy to see their dutiful regard for constructing their structures within the confines of natural phenomena, many times incorporating such things as rock outcroppings and natural terraces into the scheme of their buildings. Even shadows sometimes took on attributes of solid forms and were reckoned with by Inka architects. In such an environment, under such conditions, it is hard not to feel mystically inclined, not to be soothed by tranquil moments.

But sometimes these can be fleeting moments. In the mountains, one minute it can be crystal clear, and, in another, a plane can be enveloped desperately in clouds, with no visible fix on the ground or on the mountains that are dangerously close. It is inevitable, at moments like these, that I say to myself, "Marilyn, you've gone too far this time. This is it!" And then a patch of blue appears just before panic sets in, and you're out of the clouds. The exhilaration of the moment carries me on to the next time. I don't think that it is a question of courting danger for the sake of it. Of course, being on the edge has its adrenaline moments, but being safe is always very much on my mind. It's just that there are things out there that I want to photograph, and sometimes I have to go beyond the "reasonable" to do it.